Capital's Grave

Capital's Grave
Neofeudalism and the New Class Struggle

Jodi Dean

VERSO
London • New York

First published by Verso 2025
© Jodi Dean 2025

1 3 5 7 9 10 8 6 4 2

Verso
UK: 6 Meard Street, London W1F 0EG
US: 207 East 32nd Street, New York, NY 10016
versobooks.com

Verso is the imprint of New Left Books

ISBN-13: 978-1-80429-519-9
ISBN-13: 978-1-80429-521-2 (UK EBK)
ISBN-13: 978-1-80429-522-9 (US EBK)

British Library Cataloguing in Publication Data
A catalogue record for this book is available from the British Library

Library of Congress Cataloging-in-Publication Data

Names: Dean, Jodi, 1962- author.
Title: Capital's grave : neofeudalism and the new class struggle / Jodi
  Dean.
Description: London ; New York : Verso, 2025. | Includes bibliographical
  references and index.
Identifiers: LCCN 2024046647 (print) | LCCN 2024046648 (ebook) | ISBN
  9781804295199 (trade paperback) | ISBN 9781804295229 (US ebook) | ISBN
  9781804295212 (UK ebook)
Subjects: LCSH: Service industries workers—Social conditions. | Service
  industries—Social aspects. | Feudalism. | Capitalism. | Neoliberalism.
Classification: LCC HD8039.S45 D38 2025 (print)
  | LCC HD8039.S45 (ebook)
  | DDC 331.7/93—dc23/eng/20241123
LC record available at https://lccn.loc.gov/2024046647
LC ebook record available at https://lccn.loc.gov/2024046648

Typeset in Sabon by Biblichor Ltd, Scotland
Printed and bound by CPI Group (UK) Ltd, Croydon CR0 4YY

For Dahn and Dave, my siblings

Contents

Acknowledgments

Much has happened since I started this project: the summer 2020 protests following the murders of George Floyd, Daniel Prude, Breonna Taylor, and too many others; the deaths of over 7 million people in the COVID-19 pandemic; the January 6, 2021, assault on the US Capitol in an effort to overturn the 2020 election; the US and Israel's genocidal war against the Palestinians; and the rise of a new McCarthyism curtailing free speech and academic freedom. Sometimes the rush of events exceeded anything I was able to think or write. Other times it seemed to confirm that this violence, fragmentation, and psychosis are what neofeudalism looks like.

In my many opportunities to present early versions of this work, I benefited greatly from the questions and criticisms of multiple audiences. I appreciate the enthusiastic engagement of the students in my seminar "Capital's Futures: Becoming Neofeudal" at the European Graduate School. I am grateful to the Birkbeck Institute for the Humanities for a research fellowship and opportunities to teach in the Critical Theory Summer School, as well as to Maria Aristodemou, Elena Loizidou, Esther Leslie, and Jacqueline Rose for all they did to make this possible. Thanks to Jamie van der Klaaw for his invitation to Erasmus University in Rotterdam to participate in the Articulations of Desire conference on the state and to deliver a master class in the department of philosophy. Without the input of Matt Crow and Sarah Whitten, this project would have never gotten off the ground. Colleagues, friends, and comrades in the Nisyros Radical Critical Theory

Circle—especially my co-directors Paul Apostolidis, Albena Azmanova, Andreas Kalyvas, Regina Kreide, and Artemy Magun—were indispensable companions over the years of the project's development. Kian and Sadie Kenyon-Dean provided invaluable sources of information, inspiration, and insight. Darko Suvin was a supportive pandemic writing buddy and inspired interlocutor. Special thanks go to Jacob Powell and Kai Heron for their close critical readings of the entire manuscript. I remain grateful to Rosie Warren for crucial feedback that shaped and sharpened the book, Jeanne Tao for her careful oversight, and the support of Verso during the McCarthyism of the spring and summer of 2024. Paul Passavant read numerous drafts and expended countless hours in conversations about capitalism, feudalism, and the ways things turn out worse than we predict. His love—and the comrades who have my back—give me hope for the future and the strength to fight for it.

Introduction: Capital's Grave

One of the most powerful images in Karl Marx and Friedrich Engels's *Manifesto of the Communist Party* depicts capitalism's inevitable demise: "What the bourgeoisie therefore produces, above all, are its own gravediggers."[1] In the *Manifesto*, these gravediggers are the proletariat, the class of workers compelled to sell their labor power to survive. Exploited by the capitalist bourgeoisie, the proletarians toil in misery. They're append-ages of the machines, crowded into enormous factories and stuck in repetitive drudgery like so many cogs and pistons. The proletariat's revolutionary victory will send this unjust system to its grave. Emancipating themselves, workers will emancipate society. They will free production from the dictates of profit and manage it for the benefit of all. Classes will cease to exist, and communism will replace capitalism just as capi-talism replaced feudalism. Like the long-eclipsed knights of the sword, the knights of industry will be irrelevant figures of a bygone era, brought down by the very class they created.

The *Manifesto* inspires workers to see their struggle as one of world-historical significance. The proletariat isn't organiz-ing simply to win shorter working days and higher wages. They are fighting to transform the entire political and eco-nomic order, to end the class-division characteristic of history itself. They are fighting, and they will win. The bourgeoisie may seem powerful, but they're not invincible. Capitalist industry depends on the "revolutionary combination" of massive numbers of wage-laborers. In capitalist production, previously separated tasks and isolated workers are coordinated, concentrated, and centralized. Capital's strength is thus also its weakness: the same combined laborers on which production depends can—and will—organize to revolt against the capitalist class. Economic power will become political power. Capital will have called up the forces that bring it down.

Marx and Engels link the victory of the proletariat to the end of capitalism. Their vision remains tremendously inspiring, but it's been over 150 years since they wrote the *Manifesto* and the proletariat still hasn't won. The last half century has been an especially disheartening period of counterrevolution and defeat. Yes, there have been successful liberation struggles, revolutions, uprisings, and demonstrations. Workers resist. But no one thinks the working class is anywhere close to triumph. The defeat of the Soviet Union and global rise of neoliberalism intensified economic inequality and incited far-right nationalism around the world. Capital is winning.

McKenzie Wark challenges us to reject this conclusion.[2] She argues that capital is dead. The fact that communism has not prevailed does not mean we are still in capitalism. We're in something worse. To be honest, the first time I heard this, I thought it was nuts. It seemed perverse to deny that we live in capitalist societies. Neoliberal globalization has subjected the entire world to the dictates of capital. Communicative capitalism has changed our basic interactions into fodder for the private wealth accumulation of tech billionaires. Nonetheless, the possibility that we aren't in capitalism anymore—that the system is changing, and that we aren't acknowledging this change—continued to nag at me. Wark was onto something. Most of us recognize that history doesn't unfold in a straightforwardly progressive direction. But we still tend to assume that capitalism will continue to respond and adapt to its varying crises until we bring it down. So what if capital really is dead and its grave doesn't look anything like communism? Wark's provocation is dizzying, a call to think again about the assumptions guiding action and critique.

That capital's grave may not look anything like what Marx, Engels, and millions of their comrades anticipated pushes us to consider a further possibility: maybe its grave-diggers aren't the industrial proletariat. This is my wager and response to Wark: capital isn't dead. Capital is digging its own grave. Capitalist laws of motion are reflexively folding in on themselves and becoming something no longer recognizably capitalist. Processes long directed outward—through colonialism and imperialism—are turning inward in ways that undermine capitalist laws of motion and repeat accumulation strategies typical of feudalism: rent-seeking, plunder, and political control.

Becoming neofeudal

Many of us get our images of feudalism from popular culture— *Monty Python and the Holy Grail*, *Camelot*, *A Knight's Tale*, *The Last Duel*, *The Name of the Rose*, to use a few examples. We imagine serfs toiling in fields, vassals taking the knee, armored knights riding around with shields, swords, and lances, and monks intoning Gregorian chants in immense Gothic cathedrals. It's a European vision, seen through thick Anglo, Norman, and Teutonic fantasies that screen out regional and temporal variations within Europe as well as non-European feudalisms. We need to attend to these variations and recognize feudalism as a general economic and political formation characterized by fragmented private power and predation.

One such variation is the "democratic feudalism" that emerged in reaction to movements for political representation. Even before the French revolution, conservatives realized that they needed to harness popular energies toward the maintenance of order. Their device for doing so, Corey Robin explains, unfolded along two lines: "The masses must either

3

be able to locate themselves symbolically in the ruling class or be provided with real opportunities to become faux aristocrats in the family, the factory, or the field."[3] The first line of symbolic identification with the ruling class cultivates nationalism. The second line democratizes feudal privilege. With the home as his castle, the husband can rule over his wife. In the factory, the supervisor can feel superior to the workers beneath him. And as the United States demonstrated, slaveholding can turn "the white majority into a lordly class."[4] Facing the entry of the masses into the public sphere, conservatives entice them with private privilege: "The promise of democracy is to govern another human being as completely as a monarch governs his subjects."[5] Not only did this promise develop into an elaborate jurisprudence dedicated to fortifying private power, but it also established the contours of the conservative narration of grievance: any increase in the freedom of workers, women, and Black people deprived the lordly class of the status and honor rightfully theirs by birth.

Another variant eluding our typical view of feudalism is colonial. Confining feudalism to a European past, we forget its role in imperial conquest and exploitation, its continuity and overlap with capitalism's own development. Rahmane Idrissa's cognitive mapping of the Sahel, for example, provides a powerful description of the feudal character of colonial domination in the Sudanic region. The exclusive task of colonial political power was predation and plunder. "The parallels with a feudal order were numerous," Idrissa observes, "including a cascading system of suzerainty from the colonial *commandant* to the petty village chief, combines of chiefs and clerics as executants of customary governance, *droit du seigneur* exercised by colonial rulers, provision of security against Saharan marauders as justification for exploitation, and medieval punishments, which in some cases inspired their targets to carnivalesque religious response."[6] Idrissa emphasizes that this "feudal-style abuse" lives on in the political culture of the region, as does the "non-government" of domination. Unlike settler colonies, "exploitation colonies" such as those in the Sahel lacked the horizon of self-governance. They were peripheral hinterlands, managed from afar for the benefit of the metropole. After independence, these conditions made state formation a challenge. From the start, it was impacted by an international aid regime bent on supplying "depoliticized palliatives to pathologies that are systemic to the centre-periphery relationship."[7] Even after the destruction wrought by the debt crisis in the 1980s and neoliberalization in the 1990s, the donor class urged decentralization, ideological nonsense in a context where the state barely exists. As Idrissa points out, the subtext here is that Africa consists of tribes. The material reality is that elites don't want states getting in the way of their private interests while people living in the countryside want useful services and the enforcement of a system of impartial rules. Far from a formation confined to the European past, feudalism is a colonial arrangement with ongoing effects.

Capital's Grave isn't about feudalism, although an array of different feudalisms informs it. Since feudalism persisted long after the bourgeoisie ostensibly felled it, the book is also not evoking the return of the repressed.[8] Rather, I develop the idea of *neofeudalism* to synthesize the effects of forty years of neoliberalism: parcellated sovereignty, new lords and serfs, hinterlandization, and the everyday psychosis of catastrophic anxiety. Capitalist relations and forces of production are undergoing systemic transformation and transitioning into a different mode of production. Bringing together analyses that up till now have been dispersed in different fields—law, technology, Marxism, and psychoanalysis—I show how neofeudalism's different elements compose a single tendency marking the direction capitalism is heading.

Ellen Meiksins Wood argues that the specificity of the capitalist mode of production stems from the way market dependence compels certain forms of behavior—namely, "competition, accumulation, profit-maximization, and increasing labor productivity."[9] As a whole, the system is "uniquely driven to improve the productivity of labor by technical means."[10] I argue that the imperative of accumulation is placing capitalist laws of motion in contradiction with themselves, reshaping society and politics in the process. We are in a period of transition where profit, improvement, and competitive advantage no longer dictate accumulation strategies. Instead, rents, destruction, and hoarding combine with extra-economic coercion in a neofeudal social formation driven by privilege and dependence. Two sets of laws are operating as capitalist laws compel non-capitalist behavior.

Cédric Durand and Yanis Varoufakis offer powerful arguments for why the system in which we find ourselves is best understood as techno-feudal.[11] They bring theoretical rigor to metaphors technology writers have used for well over a decade to describe the impact of networked digital communication. In 2010, in the influential and prescient book *You Are Not a Gadget*, Jaron Lanier—who identifies as the father of virtual reality—discussed newly emergent cloud computing in terms of lords and peasants.[12] The lords own and control platforms and data. The peasants are the rest of us who have become dependent on these platforms. We may own our instruments of labor (laptops, phones, cars), but someone else—the platform lord—provides the means through which we gain access to the market, charging a fee and collecting data about our transactions. Increasingly, we don't own these items; we finance or lease them, paying not for the item but for its use. Writing just a few years after Lanier, Bruce Schneier—a network security expert—concluded a list of nefarious dealings by Facebook, Google, Apple, Microsoft, Twitter, and LinkedIn by pointing to the shift of power to IT. IT's dramatic increase in power, he said, was indicative of a "digital feudalism." Schneier warned, "If you've started to think of yourself as a hapless peasant in a *Game of Thrones* power struggle, you're more right than you realize. These are not traditional companies, and we are not traditional customers. These are feudal lords, and we are their vassals, peasants, and serfs."[13] The massive amounts of data and computing power necessary for artificial intelligence (AI) are said to be stored "in the cloud." But what is the material structure of this cloud? Servers. A few powerful tech companies own massive server farms that everyone else—companies and governments as well as individuals—pays to access. And what these servers store is us, the social substance, the general intellect, all the data that our interactions and lives generate. Really, we are the servers. Feudalism isn't just a metaphor. It's the operating system for the present.

Although often overlooked by tech writers, the neofeudalizing tendencies of communicative capitalism show up most dramatically in the servant economy. I'm not referring here to the replacement of jobs by automation but rather its opposite: the limits of automation. Jason E. Smith draws out Marx's analysis of the connection between industrialization and the expansion of services.[14] As productivity increases, requiring fewer workers, those in need of a wage to survive are thrown into sectors less amenable to automation—that is, services. Services are less amenable to automation in part because of the specific skills care work requires, skills like diapering a baby and moving an elderly person from bed. Services also resist automation because they are cheap, the last jobs available to those thrown out of every other avenue of paid employment. As Marx writes in *Capital*: "The extraordinary increase in the productivity of large-scale industry, accompanied as it is by a more intensive and a more extensive exploitation of labour-power in all other spheres of production, permits a larger and larger part of the working class to be employed unproductively. Hence it is possible to reproduce the ancient domestic slaves, on a constantly expanding scale, under the name of a servant class."[15] Marx's argument resists simplistic progressivism. Capitalist industry itself reproduces social property relations characteristic of earlier economic forms. Capital's social reproduction is not limited to the social reproduction of capitalist social relations. It can also reproduce non-capitalist social relations of servitude.

A mighty service sector has arisen over the last decades.[16] The majority of workers in the advanced economies have moved from being producers to being servants. Employed in services and retail, they assist and help. In the words of economist David Autor, "There's a lot of people who are there to serve the comfort and convenience and care of affluent individuals."[17] The COVID-19 pandemic brought out the class character of the service economy: on the one hand, people's dependence on a previously "invisible" force of warehouse and grocery workers and delivery services (with the resulting billions in profit for Amazon) and, on the other hand, the dependence of service-sector workers in bars, restaurants, hotels, tourism, personal grooming, and entertainment on the consumption patterns of the rich. When the rich stopped buying, when they retreated into their private domiciles, millions lost their livelihoods.[18] And when the rich reemerged from their mansions and penthouses, they gathered and celebrated unmasked while the servants remained masked and faceless.

Most jobs are in services, and services count for the largest areas of expected job growth. This is true all over the world. In high-income countries, 70–80 percent of employment is in services.[19] World Bank statistics for 2023 show that 54.6 percent of GDP in China comes from services, 49.8 percent of GDP in India (more than that from agriculture and industry combined), and 56.88 percent of GDP in Russia.[20] Most workers in Iran, Nigeria, Turkey, the Philippines, Mexico, Brazil, and South Africa are also in services. In every region with the exception of the Arab world (where industry continues to account for a larger share), services contribute the most to GDP: 58.28

percent in East Asia and the Pacific, 65.33 percent in Latin America and the Caribbean, and 44.41 percent in Sub-Saharan Africa.[21]

Services dominate the informal as well as the formal economy. Across what David Oks and Henry Williams call "the poor world," large percentages of workers toil in informal low-skilled service work: "The unlicensed taxi drivers, roadside fruit peddlers, freelance porters, squeegee men and women, *bidi* rollers, beggars, rag pickers, clothing resellers, small-time scammers and thieves, bazaar porters, and general-purpose unskilled jobbers who constitute the majority of the populations of cities everywhere from Kabul to Kabinda to Managua."[22] An effect of simultaneous processes of deagrarianization and deindustrialization, the production of an enormous surplus labor force enables middle-class households to employ multiple servants and insurgent militias to sweep up restless foot soldiers. Lacking access to means of subsistence, many of the people pushed into uncertain and informal service work rely on debt to survive, becoming easy prey for scammers and predatory finance.

Today, Marx's Mr. Moneybags isn't a factory owner. He's a landlord, financier, platform billionaire, or asset manager, someone who takes a cut. In the contemporary global economy, rents and predation are more effective accumulation strategies than commodity production—taking not making, as Brett Christophers explains in *Rentier Capitalism*.[23] Predation is normal, even normative. Globally, in the knowledge and tech industries, rental income accruing from intellectual property rights exceeds income from the production of goods.[24] In the US, financial services contribute more to GDP than manufacturing.[25] Increasingly, capital isn't reinvested in production. It's hoarded, given out to shareholders, or redistributed as rents to ever more powerful monopoly platforms.

Understanding the economy of rents and services as neo-feudalizing helps us make sense of the present. It lets us recognize seemingly disparate economic and social phenomena as interrelated elements of a single tendency that extends beyond the realm of high technology. Legal theorists are documenting this tendency as a privatization of jurisprudence. Robert Kuttner and Katherine Stone argue that "elites are pursuing something aptly described as a new form of feudalism, in which entire realms of public law, public property, due process, and citizen rights revert to unaccountable control by private business."[26] Kuttner and Stone's emphasis on the role of private law in erasing hard-won legal rights and protections resonates with Katharina Pistor's argument in *The Code of Capital*. Pistor describes capitalism as dependent on a feudal legal calculus: "The legal code of capitalism does not follow the rules of competition; instead, it operates according to the logic of power and privilege."[27] Privatized arbitration agreements, platform labor, social reproduction crises, and widespread feelings of pervasive, inescapable catastrophe might seem disconnected, but together they point to the result of forty years of neoliberalism: a neofeudal order with new lords and a sector of servants.

Italian theorists in the 1960s used the term *social factory* to describe the relationship between capital and labor in the postwar era. Today we inhabit a *social manor*. Society isn't oriented toward the production of workers and commodities. It's now an order of personalized service, privilege, hierarchy, and fealty. More and more of the people forced to sell their labor power to survive sell this labor as services to those looking for deliveries, drivers, cleaners, trainers, home health aides, nannies, guards, coaches, and so on. The buying and selling of services are enabled by new intermediaries, technological platforms whose owners insert themselves between service offerers and seekers, being sure to exact a fee along with the data and metadata that accompany the transaction. Our basic interactions are not our own. With advances in production seemingly at a dead end, capital is removed from circulation and transformed into assets that, however arcane, might somehow function as a store of value in an increasingly irrational and uncertain context. The privileged rely on the services of lawyers, consultants, and financial advisors to secure their hoards of value. The rest of us are supposed to stay in our place and focus on our survival. Hoping for more is naïve.

What's in a name?

Numerous terms have emerged as names for our present political-economic system. The most prominent is *neoliberalism*. When applied to domestic economies in the Global North, it's associated with post-Keynesian economic policies and the dismantling of the welfare state. When applied internationally, it's linked to globalization: globalized neoliberalism or neoliberal globalization, fancy terms to disguise intensified expropriation from the Global South. Concern with austerity—policies that cut back on state expenditures on public goods—has led to the theorization of *precarity capitalism*.[28] Christophers has added the notion of *asset manager capitalism* to his earlier analysis of *rentier capitalism*.[29] Theorists focused on technology and communication have introduced the terms *cognitive capitalism*, *digital capitalism*, *communicative capitalism*, *platform capitalism*, and *surveillance capitalism*.[30] As part of the critical examination of capitalism's responsibility for climate change, we have designations like *carbon capitalism*, *fossil capitalism*, and the *capitalocene*.[31]

These terms for present economic society accompany a slew of earlier designations that they sometimes preserve and sometimes displace: *imperialism*, *financial capitalism*, and *monopoly capitalism*. The new terms intermingle with the critical vocabulary of *racial capitalism* and *capitalist patriarchy* that aims to draw out the dependence of economic exploitation on raced and sexed oppression. They also confront the reactionary label disparaging this critique, *woke capitalism*. And all these different ways of designating contemporary capitalism coexist with claims that we've moved beyond capitalism altogether. Paul Mason, for example, suggests that our era is *post-capitalist*, and Slavoj Žižek offers *liberal communism* as the name for the elite ideology associated with Bill Gates and George Soros. Žižek presents their philanthropy as a kind of capitalist self-negation, writing: "Today's capitalism cannot reproduce on its own. It needs extra economic charity to sustain the cycle of social reproduction."[32]

Different political analyses underpin these different terms. The terms identify different sets of problems, dynamics, property relations, power relations, and sites of struggle. The most compelling theorization of neoliberalism describes it as a reactionary class response, a class project of wealth appropriation.[33] Emphases on imperialism draw out the exploitative imbrications of development and de-development as well as the necessary interconnections between liberation struggles and struggles against occupation and militarism. The different analyses also correlate to the popular struggles of the last few decades: the Movement of the Squares, the Indignados, Occupy Wall Street; struggles around austerity, cuts, and precarity; environmental struggles—not only pipelines but also prices, as in the *gilets jaunes* movement in France; housing struggles, rents, foreclosures, and evictions; Black Lives Matter, racist policing, police abolition, and struggles against occupation, apartheid, and genocide; struggles around sex, gender, sexuality, bodily autonomy, reproductive justice, and abortion. Recognizing the reactionary charge of "woke capitalism," we can even include here the struggles from below that take racist and sexist forms as they oppose immigration, vaccination, and the violation of the democratic feudal privilege of excluding or dominating another. All these struggles are over access and control, over who defines and controls who and what we are, what we get, and where we can go, in a world where capitalism cannot solve its problems—even when it controls the state—and a new formation is not yet in place.

The challenge is theorizing the connection between the crises of intensified economic inequality, social reproduction, political incapacity, and truncated political horizon (the reduction of political goals to survival and subsistence). Approaching the extremes of crisis and polarization as a struggle for democracy misrepresents the problem. *Democracy* fails to name the division in the present. For example, the rioters assaulting the US Capitol on January 6, 2021, said that they were fighting to save our democracy (when we all knew they were fascists). They mimicked the US government in its consistent undermining of other countries' democratic elections in the name of democracy. Viewing the problems of the present as an issue of democracy likewise fails to address the conditions for its absence—economic inequality, an imperialist system of exploitation that cannot be addressed through local actions, and the incapacity of existing political institutions to deal with contemporary problems. Nevertheless, the call for democracy identifies that something is missing or has been lost—but what? Popular sovereignty? Our freedom? Our future? The illusion of or desire for equality? In the civil war of contemporary society, democracy is held up in contradictory ways, to uphold the imperialist colonial order *and* to champion its abolition, to defend against fascists *and* defend against Antifa (I have in mind the bizarro world of some US Americans who glamorize the Second World War without knowing why it was fought).

If we read democracy as lost, we take the temporal perspective of a post-democratic future. If we read democracy as having never been achieved, the place from which we see is pre-democratic. The democratic expansion associated with the bourgeois revolutions didn't happen, or was foreshortened, incomplete, unfinished. A stubbornly linear Marxism-Leninism would say that pre-democracy or incomplete democracy positions us in a feudal era, the time before the democratic revolution. We're thus caught in a strange combination of temporalities. Comparisons with different historical moments illuminate different aspects of the present, which makes it hard to determine which history is repeating itself, what is tragedy and what is farce. Against this background of temporal instability, I present neofeudalism, a tendency where something new is emerging in the guise of something old.

Looking backward into the future

Medievalists argue over the meaning of *feudalism*. Some think the term is useless, a modernist effort at self-distinction.[34] The European Middle Ages lasted roughly a thousand years, comprising multiple overlapping, changing, and coexisting political and economic forms with ties and relations extending into Africa, Asia, and the Middle East. Conversely, we also have the view that "feudalism is apt to appear whenever the strain of preserving a relatively large political unit proves to be beyond the economic and psychic resources of a society."[35] From this angle, feudalism is less a mode of production than it is an effect of disintegration, a loss accompanied by combined forms of constraint and coercion imposed in order to extract surplus.

Neofeudalism isn't about the past. It's about tendencies in the present. Omnipresent feudal images and language index the challenge of understanding how our societies are changing and the difficulties we encounter in assessing continuity amid transformation. How do we see the present and identify the direction things seem to be going? There is little optimism about the future, and contemporary life is not what we were promised. Twenty years ago, people joked, "Where are the flying cars?" Now they wonder whether they will pay off their student loans or find affordable housing within a reasonable distance from their workplace. The service sector bleeds into servants bleeds into serfs trapped for life in a life they didn't choose. When the whims and consumption choices of a class of lords drive the visible economy—influencers, tech giants, strange billionaires—it registers affectively, in the feeling of hierarchy, inequality, and entrapment. Jeff Bezos has a $500 million super yacht, a yacht so big that it requires its own support yacht with a helipad. Capturing our uneasy sense of decay and decline in the context of intensifying inequality, feudal analogies critically illuminate key aspects of our contemporary experience.

In his 1973 classic *The Country and the City*, Raymond Williams analyzes the idealization of feudal values in the context of the rise of capitalist agriculture in England. A longing for the olden days, for hallowed forms of community and reciprocity, carried a critique of their displacement by self-interest and cash payment. Williams writes, "The structure of feeling within which this backward reference is to be understood is then not primarily a matter of historical explanation and analysis. What is really significant is this particular kind of reaction to the fact of change, and this has more real and more interesting social causes."[36] Locating the displaced values in the feudal past complicates their utility for social critique: Is the goal a defense of tradition, of blood and soil? If the values are in the past, what does it mean to recover them?

A risk of the neofeudalization hypothesis—the idea that capitalism is becoming neofeudal—is not idealizing feudalism (although there are some libertarians and neoreactionaries who do); rather, the risk is inadvertently defending capitalism. Against the extra-economic coercion, dependence, and violent expropriation of neofeudal pillage and plunder, capitalism may not look so bad. For example, the conservative writer Joel Kotkin uses the threat of mass serfdom to defend suburban home ownership, fossil fuels, and the American dream.[37] His neofeudal order is topped not by lords or knights but by tech oligarchs and an academic and media elite promoting a woke green ideology. Against Kotkin's mobilization of a neofeudal imaginary for a populist defense of carbon capitalism, I argue that capital itself is neofeudalizing. Capitalism isn't an alternative to neofeudalism. The drive to accumulate is transforming its own laws of motion from competition, investment, and improvement to hoarding, predation, and destruction. While destruction has always accompanied capitalist production—destruction of lives, communities, and the environment—it increasingly operates as a compulsion rather than a side effect: investors raid and dismantle functioning firms; tech start-ups aim at demolishing entire sectors; cryptocurrency-mining operations consume enormous amounts of energy while making nothing at all, cryptocurrency being the ultimate anti-commodity.[38] There's a risk, then, that neofeudalism is a conserving analytical frame, because by being worse it might make capitalism seem not to be so bad.

At the same time, neofeudalism helps account for why "class" fails to organize politics today, why left politics is so perpetually fragmented, and why the left has a hard time connecting to workers. In the so-called advanced economies, class no longer functions as a powerful political identity. The perspective of working people is not associated with an orientation to the future. The class that up through the middle of the twentieth century was able to improve its quality of life by forcing capital to make concessions has dwindled in presence and power, an effect of deindustrialization and financialization. Being a worker isn't a source of strength and pride, it's something to qualify—knowledge worker, cultural worker, tech worker—deny, or get beyond. The weakening of working-class identification is typically explained as the result of the capitalist class's sustained attack on unions. That's not wrong, but it's a forty-year-old explanation that doesn't shed much light on what's happening to workers now. According to Atlanta writer George Chidi, "People are trying very hard to avoid the word 'serf,' but that's kind of where we are."[39]

The wager behind the neofeudal hypothesis is that people have a hard time identifying as workers because they don't see their work as driving social production and collective energy, as carrying a future they believe in. Instead, they recognize it—perhaps at an inchoate or subliminal level—as serving the consumption requirements of the ruling class, a marker of feudal political economy. We work to live, while the ruling class enjoys the benefits of our labor. This recognition helps explain the prominence of identification as consumers. People use consumption choices to signal that they are more than a job: they are unique individuals with taste and talent; they belong to groups with histories that command respect. We might not make much money, but we still have our values and can cling to our guns. With consumption rather than production as the field of identity and authenticity, cultural appropriation appears as a more significant problem than exploitation; food and fashion choices become sites of generational conflict; politics concentrates around what not to buy. And because consumption is a terrain of individual expression, building collective power becomes all the more difficult, which makes it easier for the ruling class to get away with domination, destruction, and plunder.

Fighting back

Tendencies are not all determining. There is a space for, a need for, political action. We are in the setting we describe, the picture we take. Capitalism is turning itself into a neofeudal order of new lords and new serfs, platform billionaires and a massive sector of servants. Nevertheless, we can intervene. We must intervene.

Strikes and movements around the world fight back on various fronts—organizing unions, demanding an end to fossil fuels, opposing racist policing and militarism, defending women's, LGBTQ, and Palestinian liberation. The struggles of service workers are class struggles, although many of them are not at the point of production. Debt, cost of living, transportation, education, health, and housing struggles all take on the expropriative practices of asset holders. These struggles are not fought against capitalists as the bourgeois class of owners of the means of production. They are fought against landlords, banks, and the state that imposes cuts, fines, and force on the many in the interest of maintaining the power of the few. Neofeudalism is a concept that helps bring the struggles of today's proletarianized neoserfs together by showing how they are all struggles against capital's self-transformation.

Keeping the line of struggle in sight is crucial. Any argument that associates neofeudalism with the return of the repressed or some kind of repetition and regress risks falling prey to the assumption of incomplete bourgeois revolution. The corresponding path would then be toward the restoration of liberal democracy and the buttressing of capitalist class and property relations. The incessant appeal to democratic values and liberal norms goes in this direction—as if democracy were possible in neofeudalizing conditions. Such an appeal reinforces the political form of wealth expropriation while ignoring the intensification of inequality and unfreedom. The result is democracy for the rich and servitude for the many—especially in a global capitalist context where winning the state can never be enough.

A more promising line embraces services as primary labor processes in future society, holding up universal basic services (UBS) as a communist ideal alongside our traditional emphasis on the abolition of private property. On a rapidly warming planet, commodity production cannot be the central component of planned economies. Services will have to take its place, which is not just happening but accelerating. In the early months of the COVID-19 pandemic, attention to essential healthcare workers hinted at the need for and appeal of universal services before quickly shutting it down. Recognizing the labor vanguard within the array of services can link workers' and climate struggles: unionizing teachers, nurses, baristas, and hotel workers is important not only for workers' well-being but for the shape of society on a warming planet. An expanded sense of service also counters the growth and redistribution model favored in some social-democratic circles. Of course, universal basic services will have to be combined with communist goals of more free time and meaningful engagement in planning and participating in the reproduction of our common world. What's crucial to my argument is the pivotal role of services and service workers in ushering in communist society.

Given how much underpaid service work is done by noncitizen workers, the service sector is a fruitful space for international organizing. It might even be the case that emphases on care, care work, and the crisis of care point to the emergent ideology of the servant sector.[40] The value of care work ruptures capitalist value; irreducible to exchange, it points to an alternative mode of valuation, one that prioritizes maintenance, sustenance, and flourishing. Additionally, the emergent ideology of care attends to social reproduction—survival, basic needs—in ways that emphases on democracy presuppose but cannot acknowledge. With communism as the horizon, we move beyond surviving to thriving, beyond basic needs, to needs for the time and space for creativity, conviviality, exploration, and joy. Universal basic services provide the infrastructure for emancipated egalitarian forms of life.

The first chapter details capitalism's changing laws of motion. It uses Uber and the *Grundrisse* to show what's distinctive about neofeudalism. Chapter 2 sets out the temporality of neofeudalism, thinking through the logic of transition and demonstrating how the Marxist tradition always had a richer, more varied understanding of time than the straightforward parade of stages suggests. The third chapter describes the state, class, spatial, and affective structure of neofeudalism, emphasizing parcellated sovereignty, new lords and serfs, hinterlandization, and catastrophic anxiety. Chapter 4 takes up the psychotic atmosphere pervading neofeudalism, reflecting on the ubiquitous sentiment that "nobody cares." I conclude with a vision for class struggle on a warming planet and led by a servant vanguard. We aren't doomed to neofeudal stagnation and servitude. A better world is possible, if we fight for it.

1

What the *Grundrisse* Tells Us about Uber

At a rally in 2019, California Assembly Speaker Anthony Rendon announced, "When you hear about folks talking about the new economy, the gig economy, the innovation economy, it's fucking feudalism all over again."[1] Rendon was there to support legislation classifying most gig workers as employees rather than as independent contractors. Assembly Bill 5 was intended to bring gig workers under the protection of existing California labor laws, and the bill passed. But the following year, California voters chose feudalism: they approved Proposition 22, a ballot measure heavily funded by Uber, Lyft, DoorDash, and Instacart that would exempt app-based drivers from the labor protections that Assembly Bill 5 tried to secure. The apps won. And what they won was access to a labor force liberated from employment protection.

Neoliberal capitalism has been a period of working-class defeat. Neofeudalism arises from that defeat. Practices and policies designed to protect the class position and accumulation strategies of asset holders, to preserve their wealth and grip on the social surplus, are impacting capital's laws of motion. We live in a period of transition where capital is undermining its own conditions and becoming neofeudal.

Ellen Meiksins Wood explains that capitalism is "a specific social form, with a distinctive social structure and distinctive social relations of production, which compel economic agents to behave in specific ways and generate specific laws of motion."[2] This of course isn't a definition of capitalism; it tells us what a definition has to encompass. We can't define capitalism—or any specific social form—just by listing its features. We have to figure out its dynamics, how its elements relate to and affect one another. Social property relations compel behaviors that follow specific patterns, their "laws of motion." The split between owners and workers and the mediation of their relation through the market generate capitalism's specific laws of motion: "the *imperatives* of competition and profit-maximization, a *compulsion* to reinvest surpluses, and a systematic and relentless *need* to improve labor-productivity and develop the forces of production."[3] I'm interested in how these laws of motion are coming into conflict with each other. Imperatives of competition can lead not just to monopoly but to conquest. The drive to maximize profits can prevent the reinvestment of surpluses in production, directing them toward destruction instead. Capitalism's own laws can turn in on themselves, undermine capitalism, and follow neofeudal dynamics of rent-seeking, predation, and plunder.

A tendency, not a fad

Capitalism has always been immiserating—"accumulation of misery a necessary condition, corresponding to the accumulation of wealth," as Marx puts it.[4] What, then, does neofeudalism add? Evgeny Morozov's critique of techno-feudalism helps us explore this question.

Morozov dismisses feudal references as meme-hungry intellectual laziness, failures to understand digital capitalism rather than insights alert to the possibility that capitalism might be transitioning into a political and economic form no longer aptly described as capitalist.[5] Might references to neo- or techno-feudalism be covertly conservative, a sneaky way of saying that capitalism is not so bad and therefore we should do everything we can to shore it up? Responding to Morozov's criticisms, Cédric Durand puts these insinuations to bed: if commodity production continues to drive capital accumulation, then the Marxist critique remains appropriate; if, however, accumulation depends on rents, predation, and plunder, then attention to neofeudalizing tendencies "will allow us to grasp and fight the emerging forms of social domination."[6] And, we might add, both can be true at the same time—periods of transition in particular are marked by the overlap of competing forms and logics.

Morozov's critique is nonetheless useful in its pinpointing of the role of "extra-economic coercion" in capital accumulation. Is capitalism unthinkable in the absence of violence, or is capitalism an economic system with a logic irreducible to violence? Getting clarity on these questions is crucial for any account of neofeudalism. We can't understand what capitalism might be changing itself into if we can't say what is distinctive about capitalism. For Morozov, the alternatives are between the definition offered by Marxists like Robert Brenner and Ellen Meiksins Wood and that offered by Immanuel Wallerstein's world systems theory. Marxists generally conceive feudalism as expropriation driven by extra-economic coercive or political means: lords expropriate surplus from peasants over whom they exercise juridical power. Capitalism differs in that it is a relation of exploitation. Surplus is extracted by economic means: deprived of the means of subsistence, nominally free workers are obliged to sell their labor power for a wage in order to survive in a cash economy. In contrast, Wallerstein argues that capitalism also relies on extra-economic coercion, most profoundly the core's expropriation of surplus from the periphery. Morozov sides with Wallerstein. He faults accounts such as Brenner's and Wood's for too narrowly conceiving capitalism in terms of the laws of motion arising from specific social property relations that compel innovations in production. Morozov thinks that this narrow conception leads Brenner and Wood to consign a whole slew of activities necessary for accumulation to a separate political sphere, preventing them from acknowledging the inextricability of racism, patriarchy, colonialism, and state violence from capitalism. More broadly, he argues that exploitation-centric approaches to capitalism are pushed to employ extraneous concepts like predation, dispossession, extraction, rentierism, and neofeudalism in order to understand the present. Wouldn't it be more accurate simply to expand our understanding of capitalism?

If capitalist exploitation is unthinkable apart from expropriation, if it is inextricable from violent taking, then the primary difference between capitalism and feudalism breaks down. By claiming this breakdown for capitalism, Morozov forfeits the ability to distinguish it from feudalism; there isn't a difference between the modes of production that matters. This is hardly a conceptual advance; it rejects the fundamental premise of Marx's entire project. Taking—seizure, pillage, plunder—is redistribution, not production. Likewise, heaps of accumulated wealth are not in themselves capital. Capital is a relation, a relation not identical with brute force. As William Clare Roberts underscores, "Violence and theft cannot give rise to capital directly. There must be a displacement from the acts of violence and theft to the process of capitalizing upon the conditions thereby created."[7] That capitalism is historically accompanied and reinforced by coercion does not make capitalist processes indistinguishable from direct and violent expropriation. One could just as easily claim the breakdown of the conceptual distinction between capitalism and feudalism for feudalism: insofar as accumulation has never not involved violent expropriation, we have never been capitalists. Feudalism never ended.

To be sure, feudalism as expropriation is not the whole of the Marxist story: extra-economic coercion isn't simply replaced by exploitation. It accompanies it. Capital comes to overlay, incorporate, and rely on previous economic and social forms. As chapter 2 explains, Marx was attuned to the coexistence of different modes of production. His distinction between formal and real subsumption mobilizes this coexistence. Western Marxists' preoccupation with the "completed process" of real subsumption—that is, with technical improvement in labor productivity has led to the neglect of capital's continuous encounter with and absorption of non-capitalist elements, the process of formal subsumption.[8] What Morozov presents as a necessary but as yet undeveloped model of capitalism bringing together expropriation and exploitation is already present in Marx, and not simply in the origin story of primitive accumulation but more centrally and profoundly in the continuous process of formal subsumption whereby capitalism metabolizes its exterior. Formal subsumption points to capitalism's dependence on elements it absorbs but doesn't generate, elements produced through any number of non-capitalist labor processes.

Morozov emphasizes that "dispossession and expropriation have been constitutive of accumulation throughout history."[9] His dissolution of the difference between feudalism and capitalism in favor of eternal expropriation fails to attend to changes in the forms of exploitation. He naturalizes capitalism in a way already effectively criticized by Wood.[10] And he abandons any effort to recognize and specify system change. Marx understood that the compulsion to perform surplus labor is not unique to capitalism. Pre-capitalist economic formations associated with communal ownership such as slavery and serfdom (and of course Marx recognized the existence of both these forms of exploitation under capitalism) also compel labor to produce a surplus that the master and the lord expropriate. Capitalism changes the form of this compulsion. What was a direct and personal form of domination becomes impersonal domination mediated by the market. Market pressures induce owners to find ways to get workers to do more, work harder, produce more surplus value. The question of neofeudalism and neo-feudalization is whether we are seeing another change in form.

For Morozov, "capitalism is moving in the same direction it always has been."[11] But might not movement in the same direction lead to falling off a cliff? Or put in the old-fashioned terms of dialectical materialism, can't quantity turn into quality? Although Morozov doesn't explain what he means by capitalism's direction, his gesture to the neofeudalism discussion as "making the strange argument that capitalism is somehow moving in reverse" suggests that he presumes a linear, progressivist notion of history.[12] Conceivably, we're already at the end of history, since capitalism is infinitely adaptable. All that will ever happen is variations on the same. What Morozov fails to consider is whether capitalism's own dynamics can transform it into something else, something worse, something we need to identify and oppose.

Inequality

Recent work by non-Marxist as well as Marxist scholars brings out the dynamics underlying neofeudalism. The data sets and categories of analysis differ, but they point to the same combination of intensified inequality and accumulation uncoupled from production.

In his famous 2014 book, *Capital in the Twenty-First Century*, Thomas Piketty demonstrates that wealth inequality increases under capitalism because the rate of return on capital is higher than the rate of economic growth. Simply put, wealth accumulates at a rate higher than the rate at which wages rise. Since few people have significant wealth, since wealth is concentrated in the hands of the few, the distance between those with wealth and those reliant on earned income expands. The expression "rate of return on capital" points to the rents that can be extracted from existing assets. "Rent" refers to more than the payment demanded by monopoly control over land—in other words, what landlords make us pay.

It includes the fee or payment commanded by monopoly control over any asset—for example, financial instruments, digital platforms, and intellectual property.

Brett Christophers presents "rentier capitalism" as a system "not just dominated by rents and rentiers but, in a much more profound sense, substantially scaffolded by and organized around the assets that generate those rents and sustain those rentiers."[13] The ethos of a system where rentier relations predominate is "proprietorial rather than entrepreneurial."[14] Accumulated wealth generates more accumulated wealth and pushes a reshaping of the economic system toward accumulated wealth; that is to say, rents—taking rather than making.

Robert Brenner offers a different but compatible explanation for the intensification of inequality—the declining rate of profit. Since the 1970s, capital's growing difficulty in generating profit by investing in means of production (plants and equipment) and employing workers to make commodities has led it to pursue alternative accumulation strategies. The one Brenner highlights is the "upward redistribution of wealth through political means."[15] Rather than operating as capitalists who acquire wealth by investing in production, the already wealthy pursue political strategies to force social wealth up to themselves. These strategies don't involve seeking advantages that will give them a competitive edge. They aren't about growing the economy or baking a bigger pie. They're about taking a bigger piece. Pointing out the error involved in reading neoliberalism as an intensification of competition, Brenner argues that "what's essential here is the opposite of competitiveness: It is access to special privileges that directly yield wealth, thanks to political position or connection."[16] Bluntly put, the players aren't winning in the markets; they are using "extra-economic power" to change the game. The accumulation strategy is political. Brenner lists tax cuts, privatization, intellectual property, failure to enforce laws against monopoly, wealthy people collecting interest on government debt (which increases because the government finances itself by debt rather than taxes), and the "rise of the financial sector, which is no doubt the main base of the new political economy of upwardly distributing wealth through political means."[17] Rather than simply using political means to acquire competitive advantage in the markets, the wealthy use political means for their own direct enrichment. Firms get privileges (loans, loopholes, low interest rates, low liquidity requirements, and so on) and politicians get campaign contributions (greatly facilitated by the Supreme Court's ruling in *Citizens United*)—and then positions in firms or on corporate boards whose officers will also get political appointments (Goldman Sachs seems virtually guaranteed a top position in the US Treasury Department). The US economy is based on plunder, predation, and hoarding, as should be clear to everyone since at least 2008, when bailouts of the big banks were handed out absent any measures to hold them accountable or prevent the sort of speculation that led to the disaster in the first place.

The dynamics here are global. The rate of economic growth is slowing down across the capitalist system. The delinking of capital accumulation from production is a general phenomenon in a system with players who have enormous differences in strength, wealth, technology, and capacity. When some win, others lose. For example, China's economic growth in the first decades of the twentieth century occurred in a context of low rates of worldwide economic growth. The market share of Chinese firms increased, while that of other countries—the US, Brazil, Mexico, and South Africa—declined.[18] Accompanying China's industrial success, and compounded by its economic slowdown around 2013, was the deindustrialization of poor and middle-income countries throughout the world.[19] Already facing deagrarianization, severe indebtedness, and weakened state capacity as a result of structural adjustment policies, countries such as Argentina, Brazil, Iraq, Nigeria, and Venezuela decomplexified their economies and resorted to exporting raw commodities, particularly natural resources like oil and gas. While commodity prices were high, these exports could fund significant poverty-reduction measures. In states without the requisite popular mobilization and political will, export proceeds fed the luxury consumption of elites.[20] When prices dropped, millions were pushed into insecure, informal service work.

Capitalism produces inequality. Across the globe, holders of capital pressure states to facilitate and protect their seizure of the social product. Rather than investing in production, holders of capital hoard their assets. Corporations buy back stocks and reward their executives, in effect feeding the consumption of the rich instead of putting money into improvements, growth, or the labor force. It's worth noting that the lords' consumption was a primary driver in the European feudal economy and, for some analysts, a primary explanation for its relative stagnation. At any rate, with the intensification of private equity and leveraged buyouts, much of the investment that occurs today is oriented toward conquest and destruction, the over-celebrated "disruption" of entire economic sectors. Capitalism's dynamics are neofeudalizing, transitioning into an economic system that no longer follows capitalist laws of motion.

Uber

As everybody knows, Uber is a ride-sharing app that lets people use their phones to order a car and driver that will usually cost less and arrive sooner than a taxi. Conversely, the app enables car owners or renters to gain access to ride-seekers, connecting them to the market. Uber collects a fee for this service.

Uber describes its service as providing a tool for people to earn extra cash by driving in their spare time. Instead of their private car just sitting in their driveway, it's put to use, helping people get to where they need to go and benefiting their owners at the same time. Uber considers the drivers who use the app to be independent contractors accessing "flexible earning opportunities." A company white paper explains that:

> Flexibility allows people to choose if, when, where, for whom and for how long they work. This means that, unlike traditional employment relationships, offering their service via platforms like Uber can fit around a person's other priorities—whether that be caring for a child or loved one, studying, or combining multiple earning opportunities at the same time. This provides access to earning opportunities for people who often find themselves excluded from the labour market.[21]

Uber's propaganda presents the company as liberating people from the tyranny of traditional employment by giving them new ways to access income. It frees people to work independently.

In February 2021, a UK employment court rejected Uber's claims that drivers using the app are independent contractors. It held that Uber drivers are employees. The opinion observed that, unlike independent contractors, employed workers are in a position of subordination and dependency; employers control their "working conditions and remuneration."[22] Uber drivers have no say in their contracts with Uber. Uber controls the information drivers receive: drivers don't know the destination until they pick up the rider. Uber decides how much drivers can charge for a ride and how large a service fee it will extract. Uber monitors drivers' acceptances, cancellations, and passenger rates, penalizing them up to the point of kicking them off the app if they don't conform to the standards Uber sets. Since Uber clearly controls drivers' working conditions and remuneration, it's no surprise that the employment court determined them to be employed workers entitled to legally guaranteed rights of a minimum wage, pension, and paid vacation.

In California, Uber drivers remain independent contractors—the result of a battle waged by Uber and others. Uber, Lyft, DoorDash, and Instacart shoveled over $220 million into the Prop 22 ballot measure exempting drivers from employee benefits. In the campaign leading up to the vote, Uber emphasized flexibility. It even built into the app some flexibility options that would let drivers set their own fares (the multiplier) and see the destination before accepting a ride. Less than a year after the passage of Prop 22, Uber removed those features from the app. It also substantially decreased fares from Los Angeles International Airport (LAX). Nevertheless, in March 2023 a state appellate court upheld Prop 22.[23]

According to Uber driver Tonje Ettesvoll, "A lot of drivers were very gung-ho about Proposition 22."[24] Their support wasn't unfounded. Some valued being able to set their own work times. Over and over again, drivers say that flexibility is a priority (and this response appears even in research not sponsored by Uber). In the run-up to the Prop 22 vote, there were drivers who reported that they wanted the protections offered to employees, but they feared the power Uber could have over them as their employer. In the words of Nina, a fifty-year-old Venezuelan immigrant driving for Uber and Lyft in San Francisco:

Of course, I want to be an employee, but on the other hand, I think, how would I be treated by Travis Kalanick, as him being my employer? He would have a whip on us. What is he going to do to me as an employee? I know he is capable of many things. This man is an awful man, awful to the point that I think he is a sociopath. And to have so many people feeding families in the hands of a sociopath is bad. Uber is so ruthless to these software engineers. Imagine what they would do to us [drivers].[25]

Still other drivers doubted that Uber would provide them with benefits even if they were classified as employees. To them, Uber feels above or beyond the law, able to evade it. In the face of the wealth, power, and relentlessness of companies like Uber, law is but a cardboard shield offering no real protection. Fear of Uber and its founder makes particular sense given Uber's corporate culture. Under Kalanick, the company pursued growth at any cost, seeking "nothing less than utter domination," the "obliteration of any opponent," "a complete monopoly."[26] Prior to his ouster in 2017, Kalanick was known internally to refer to drivers as "supply."[27] They weren't even people.

Laws, particularly local regulations around taxi and livery services, got in Kalanick's way. But they didn't stop him. To establish itself in a city, the company would spend millions on incentives for drivers and free rides for customers, more than $2 billion annually by 2015.[28] Regulators would realize that their city's taxi service was under assault only after Uber had become too popular for city officials to reign it back in.[29] Philadelphia is a good example: Uber came into the market illegally, was fined $12 million for over 120,000 violations of the transit code, settled these fines for $3.5 million—and remained in the city.[30] The company relies on hundreds of lobbyists, more than Amazon, Microsoft, and Walmart combined.[31] Uber's enormous incentive and lobbying campaign isn't funded by profits; it didn't make any profit until 2023. Before going public, Uber raised the capital required for its rapid expansion—$24.5 billion—over the course of twelve funding rounds. Investors threw huge stores of accumulated capital at Uber in the hope of profiting from the forced deregulation of urban transport and the resulting dramatic reduction in drivers' pay.

Innovation is typically seen as one of the advantages of the capitalist mode of production. Capitalist laws of motion are supposed to impel improvements in labor productivity. Uber has not improved efficiency in the urban transportation sector. Writing in 2016, transportation economist Hubert Horan observed that Uber was the most highly valued private company in the world (at the time the company's venture capital valuation was $69 billion).[32] But the company was losing more money than any start-up in history. It was growing because the massive influx of venture capital let it subsidize rides (passengers paid less than the cost of their trips) and drive other car services out of business. Uber's strategy was predatory, taking control of a sector rather than improving it. Horan writes,

> In the hundred years since the first motorized taxi, there has been no evidence of significant scale economies in the urban car service industry . . . Drivers, vehicles, and fuel account for 85% of urban car service costs. None of these costs decline significantly as companies grow . . . Uber has not discovered a magical new way to drive down unit costs.

Uber's goal was never improvement; it was conquest. As a result, driver pay has declined by more than 40 percent; in some cities drivers are now working below minimum wage.[33]

Commentators describe the destructive impact of Uber and similar platforms in various ways. For some, Uber exemplifies "algorithmic management," a digitally turbocharged Taylorism.[34] Others see it as installing "a modern version of the company town."[35] Still others highlight the creation of a "new form of servant, one distributed through complex markets to thousands of different people."[36] Billions in venture capital fund the development of "on-demand servant services."[37] These billions produce the conditions that reduce some to servitude while elevating others. Juliet B. Schor writes, "An insidious aspect of labor platforms is that they are essentially recreating a servant economy."[38] Uber drives down wages in the urban transportation sector, subsidizing passengers' rides while making it impossible for most drivers to earn a living wage. It pushes some into debt as they finance the cars they need to drive in order to earn. Airbnb has led to declines in hotel revenue, employee layoffs, and shortages in affordable housing. DoorDash not only relies on Uber's grossly underpaid independent contractor model but threatens the restaurant sector by stimulating the emergence of "ghost restaurants"—unlicensed, uninspected kitchens that reproduce the menus of actual restaurants for the purpose of delivery.[39]

At first glance, these interpretations of platforms like Uber conflict with each other. The perspective seems to be that of either unbridled capitalism or the servitude of a new feudalism. This opposition repeats the either-or of employee or independent contractor. Strangely, though, the binaries are inverted. For defenders of the designation "employee," it is better for drivers to be workers under capitalist employers than it is for them to be independent contractors. Legally regulated conditions of employment—won by decades of working-class struggle—protect employees from the despotic compulsion of capitalists to work them more and pay them less. Defenders of the "independent contractor" designation—including many drivers and other gig workers—don't see employee status as liberating. These workers say that they value their freedom to set their own schedules, to work on their own terms. They loathe how Uber manipulates its app in ways that make them unfree, but this does not mean that they want to be employees. Likewise, from the Uber side, the platform side, we have a scenario where the ostensible capitalist doesn't want to be a capitalist—that is, doesn't want to invest in means of production and purchase labor power. Platform workers don't work for a wage. As Uber says, drivers perform a service payment from which the platform extracts a fee, rent. The customer or passenger hires and pays a driver. The

driver is free to work at will, so long as the app gets its cut—
the price of labor's emancipation.

The *Grundrisse*

In the *Grundrisse* we find another story of free and unfree
labor: Marx's account of the separation of the worker from
communal-based forms of property in land and labor. Marx is
explaining the historicity of capital, how capitalism didn't
create the conditions out of which it arises but instead changes
these conditions through its emergence. There were productive relations before the development of capitalism. People
reproduced themselves and their communities in ways that
were non-capitalist, that involved securing basic subsistence
and meeting social needs. Capitalism comes out of and transforms these prior relations. What, then, did these pre-capitalist
relations look like? What forms did they take? Since capitalism has not always existed, its key elements of free workers
and accumulated capital cannot themselves be products of
capital. So what sort of relations do we have to assume capitalism to have negated?

Marx posits an originary unity of the producer with the
land, a unity mediated by membership in a community. In this
ancient communal form, the producer is a proprietor. The
proprietor takes for granted that the earth and soil are there
for him to labor on in order to reproduce himself, to live. The
premise of these original conditions of production is the individual's existence as part of a social group. "In this community,
the objective being of the individual as proprietor, say proprietor of land, is presupposed, and presupposed moreover under
certain conditions which chain him to the community, or
rather form a link in his chain."[40] Land belongs to proprietors
only to the extent that it and they belong to the community. In

fact, it's really the community that's the "force of production."[41] Nature and social group, earth and commune, form objective conditions for the producers' reproduction.

Capital presupposes the dissolution of this originary unity, what Marx describes as a historic process of separation. *Capital* tells a story of violent enclosure, bloody expropriation, and the brutal creation of a vagabond mass. The *Grundrisse* presents an unfolding where the processes through which the community of proprietors reproduce themselves are also processes of production and destruction. To reproduce themselves, proprietors engage in production. Through production they reproduce themselves and their social relations. In turn, this production works back on the proprietors, changing them and their social relations. Increases in population require the clearing of more wilderness and cultivation of more land. The need for more land propels conquest and colonization. As communities increase in size, the strength of the ties between members decreases. Urban separates from rural. Accompanying the rise of towns is the development of artisanal craft labor with property in the instruments of labor becoming distinct from landed property. Just as property in land is presumed to belong to the producer, so is property in his own labor and the products of his labor presumed to belong to the artisan. And just as the commune is the presumed social basis of landed property, so is the guild the communal basis for artisanal property in labor.

What these two forms of property in land and in labor share is that in each instance the proprietors of land and labor have means of subsistence in their possession before production takes place. The producer isn't waiting on someone to pay him so that he can buy what he needs to live. That the landed proprietor is "directly provided with the necessary consumption fund" is clear. Marx argues that artisanal labor presupposes a similar access to necessities. Viewing craftwork as occurring within guilds and journeymen craftsmen as apprenticed to a master, he explains that the apprentice "does not appear as an actual independent worker at all, but shares in the master's fare in a patriarchal way."[42] The guild-master's consumption fund supports the apprentice working under him.

The rise of artisanal labor and property in the instruments of labor brings about a loosening, a separation, in the community. The community starts to appear differently, not as a naturally and spontaneously given relation to land but as itself a product of labor. Craftworkers create guilds. An emergent feature of increasing urbanization, the guild system is the product of worker-owners, of those who own the instruments of their labor. Marx argues that because the element that constitutes property—the instrument—is posited by labor, the community itself appears as made, "produced by the worker himself."[43]

Not every producer is a proprietor; not every worker is an owner. Marx describes slavery and serfdom as secondary but logically necessary results of "property founded upon the community and upon labor in the community."[44] They follow from these earlier relations of property in land and labor, and constitute an element of the "development and decay" of these relations.[45] In slavery and serfdom, "one part of society is treated by the other as itself merely an inorganic and natural condition of its own reproduction."[46] From the perspective of the proprietors, slaves and serfs are like land, animals, and tools. Marx thus sees in slavery and serfdom a third form of relation to the means of subsistence. If the first was proprie-torship over land and the second proprietorship over labor and instruments, two forms of worker-ownership, then this third form entails a shift from the side of owning to the side of being owned, from having property to being property. Describing "the relation of retainers to their lords," Marx explains that personal service "forms at bottom merely the mode of existence of the landowner, who no longer labors himself, but whose property includes the laborers themselves as serfs, etc., among the conditions of production. What we have here as an essential relation of appropriation is the *relationship of domination*."[47] These relationships of domination do not deprive slaves and serfs of means of subsistence; their means of subsistence is the property of another, through whom they access it. Slaves and serfs are means of subsistence and partake from another's means of subsistence. Slavery and serfdom, then, are forms of domination that don't contradict the positing of an originary unity, because the slave and serf exist as extensions of the master and the lord, tied to labor and land. Nevertheless, these practices point to the fact of negation and change, to the ways that the originary unity becomes something else, conditions for the possibility of capitalism.

The premise of capital is that the whole has dissolved into parts. Work and ownership separate from each other. The proprietor of the land no longer works the land. Those who work the land no longer own it. Craftworkers stop owning the instruments of labor. The tools employ them.[48] As Marx says in *Theories of Surplus Value*: "The *means of production*, the material conditions of labor—material of labor, instruments of labor (and means of subsistence)—do not appear as subsumed to the laborer, but the laborer appears as subsumed to them. He does not make use of them, but they make use of him."[49] And although serfdom and slavery are also present under capitalism, the capital relation itself posits their negation. The capitalist doesn't own the workers. He purchases their labor power.

"Historic processes" of reproduction generated conditions that separated producers from the means of subsistence that sustained them. Once separated, their lack of property in land and the instruments of labor forces them to find other ways to access what they need to survive. With the coercive authority of the state blocking some avenues of acquisition, many turn to the wage, selling their labor power in order to acquire what they need to survive. Their productive labor is not for the sake of use, but for the sake of exchange. Rather than being embedded in a communal world where the objective conditions of production—land, raw materials, tools, and means of subsistence—are taken for granted, workers confront these conditions as alien and external. These conditions are still present, Marx tells us, "but in another form; as a *free fund*, in which all political, etc. relations are obliterated. The objective conditions of labor now confront these unbound, propertyless individuals only in the form of *values*, self-sufficient values."[50] Labor's conditions lose their political character as elements given by communal life and as relations premised on direct, personal domination. Separated out from the laborers, "freed" from their proprietorship, these conditions are available for purchase, just as the labor power of the workers is available for a wage. Everything that was present in the originary unity is still there, but in a different form. In this new form, the separated conditions of production come together through the mediation of the market.

Free and unfree workers

Marx uses *free* in the sense of unencumbered, disconnected. "Free" workers are those to whom land and their own labor no longer belong, those free of proprietorship. He describes the mass of living labor thrown onto the market as "free in a double sense, free from the old relations of clientship, bondage, and servitude, and secondly free of all belongings and possessions, and of every objective, material form of being, *free of all property*."[51] Marx's description gives us a way to understand why it actually makes sense to think of Uber drivers as independent contractors. Not because of what they gain through the app—flexibility, a way to be their own boss, control over their working conditions—but because of what they lose. They are freed from the rights of employees—guaranteed working hours, some modicum of paid leave, healthcare benefits. They are also further freed of their property in that an item that had belonged to them, their car, takes on a new form, that of an instrument for the capital accumulation of another.

Let's look more closely at these two sides of Uber drivers' freedom. On the one hand, their freedom from the status of employee enables them to think of themselves as independent contractors; they work when they choose. Whether they are out there driving and earning is a matter of their own will. They have not sold their labor power to Uber as an employer. The Uber app connects them to buyers, ride-seekers, for a fee. Drivers sell transport services to potential passengers. Marx says that "the relation between buyer and seller of this *service* has nothing to do with the relation of the productive laborer to capital."[52] The buyer of the ride service is not employing the driver in order to accumulate capital by putting them to work. The seller of the service, the driver, is not being put to work on means of production owned by the buyer. The instrument of labor, the car, belongs to the driver (below I consider going into debt in order to have a car to drive). The driver is in a proprietary relation with the car. Like the craftsman whose skill and instrument are his own, rather than means of production owned by a capitalist, so too does the car belong to the driver.

And yet something in the driver's relationship to their car changes: from being an item of consumption—something they either purchased out of their own consumption fund, wages they had received for their labor, or something which someone else purchased for them out of their consumption fund—the car becomes a means for the accumulation of another, Uber. Instead of Uber paying for and maintaining a fleet of cars, the company puts others' cars to use, in effect getting cars to employ their owners. An item of consumption is transformed into an instrument of production. Here, then, is the other hand, the car's change in form: as a vehicle for Uber's extraction of a fee, what had been something belonging to the worker loses its prior status. This is true in a material sense: Uber requires that vehicles are under fifteen years old and have seat belts and four doors. Because they are rated by riders, many drivers feel pressured to keep their cars extra clean and pleasant smelling, sometimes even stocked with water and treats, in ways they never would when driving for themselves. Through Uber, the car owner is separated from their prior relation to the object. Their relation to the object changes from a consumptive relation to a productive relation. The purpose is less personal enjoyment than generation of income. Their car is now an instrument for putting them to work. It stands apart from its owner as an independent value. The car becomes capital.

The debt some go into in order to drive is the extreme that demonstrates the truth of the car's change in form. Debt tethers drivers to the platform. Drivers bear the entire burden of car maintenance. This is an expected consumption expense, part of enjoying the benefits of a vehicle of one's own. Uber turns this expected consumption expense into a cost of production, which drivers assume. Describing the "artificial power" (non-market, extra-economic) Uber accrues by shifting vehicle costs onto drivers, Horan writes, "Traditional cab drivers could easily move to other jobs if they were unhappy, but Uber's drivers were locked into vehicle financial obligations that made it much more difficult to leave once they discovered how poor actual pay and conditions were."[53] To drive, drivers must keep their car in good repair. To pay for repairs, drivers must drive, which means earning for Uber as well as themselves. Some drivers have to drive in order to make their car payments, and those who made sure their cars met Uber's specifications have even higher payments. Newer-model vehicles may have remote activation features; drivers who don't keep up on their payments can have their cars "remotely deactivated then repossessed."[54] As Uber increases its service fee, as more drivers use the app, as Uber employs various quota measures to regulate the number and quality of drivers, drivers' income is threatened. They have to work more and more hours, make themselves available for more and more rides, to maintain their prior pay. What was supposed to be flexible becomes a new form of serfdom, app bondage.

Drivers' double freedom from employee status and from their own consumer item (the car's change in form) ushers in a double dependence, dependence on the market and dependence on Uber for access to the market. Under capitalism, work is distributed through a labor market. It isn't given, present, assumed as a dimension of social membership. Workers have to secure it, under better or worse conditions. Once they've secured employment, workers sell their labor power to employers for a period of time determined by a contract. Typically, the employers are capitalists who purchase labor power as a strategy for accumulating capital. Independent contractors are generally not employed by capitalists as part of the process of production but by customers as part of these customers' consumption. Despite these differences with respect to who purchases labor power and for what purpose, both workers seeking employment and independent contractors depend on the labor market. This is the first dimension of dependence. It's the addition of a second dimension of dependence on Uber—or any such platform—for access to the market that distinguishes drivers from typical workers under capitalism. Uber inserts itself between driver and rider. They cannot meet without Uber, so they're dependent not just on the market but on the platform as well.

Uber's insertion of itself as an intermediary between buyer and seller resembles Marx's discussion of the merchant who transforms independent spinners and weavers into dependent workers. The merchant restricts them "little by little to

one kind of work in which they become dependent on selling, on the *buyer*, the *merchant*, and ultimately produce only
through him."⁵⁵ This resemblance is merely superficial. For
one, Uber differs from the merchant in that it is not the buyer.
Although drivers drive through Uber, Uber isn't buying their
labor power; riders are paying for labor. For another, the
merchant acts in a market and is subject to market imperatives. In contrast, Uber destroys the market. It's a mediator
that destroys what it ostensibly mediates. By offering drivers
financial incentives to start driving and offering riders
cheaper, subsidized rides to get started, Uber disrupts the
urban transport market. The various regulations cities have
long used to keep urban transportation costs reasonably
stable and ensure that rides even to inconvenient places stay
somewhat reliable are forcibly demolished. Uber's control
over access to the market enables it to control those dependent on access to the market. Because drivers must earn to live,
they have no choice but to pay the fees and submit to their
bondage to the app. They're trapped in a new kind of serfdom.

Uber's own propaganda presents the app as enabling drivers to combine "multiple earning opportunities at the same
time" and providing "access to earning opportunities for
people who often find themselves excluded from the labor
market." Why would people need to combine multiple earning opportunities? Because a single "opportunity" doesn't
provide sufficient income. Why would people find themselves
excluded from the labor market? According to Horan, 90
percent of app-based drivers in New York City are recent
immigrants, most of whom are from Haiti, the Dominican
Republic, Pakistan, India, and Bangladesh. This suggests an
exclusion from the labor market based on immigration status
linked to imperialism and climate change. Additional reasons
for exclusion could include massive layoffs, unemployment,
the evisceration of an economic sector. Changes in the labor
market themselves throw people out of it, failing to allocate

labor in ways that enable people to secure their means of subsistence.

Marx describes capital as reliant on the reserve army of the unemployed that it produces. Kalanick, since he wasn't seeking employees, called these people "supply." Uber is premised on this supply. Its demolition of urban transport is crucial to its accumulation strategy: it doesn't compete by improving; it destroys other options for riders and drivers. Its fee increases and manipulation of its algorithm to reward drivers who are always on and punish drivers who don't make certain quotas further contribute to "supply" by forcing drivers to work more for less. This isn't capitalist exploitation; it's neofeudal expropriation.

Conquest and destruction

Platform work in general carries out this sort of destruction wherever it takes hold. Companies like Uber, Lyft, Grubhub, DoorDash, and Instacart have "rearranged the way people get basics tasks done, and they've wired those in local industries—handymen, house cleaners, dog walkers, dry cleaners—into the tech- and capital-rich global economy. These people are now submitting to a new middleman, who they know controls the customer relationship and will eventually have to take a big cut, as Uber drivers would be happy to tell them."[56] Workers who have earned by providing customers with services are being absorbed by platforms. Where before their earnings were their own, now an intermediary exacts a fee, a rent based on control over access to the market. The inability to escape fees entraps more than individuals. Strong companies turn weaker or dependent ones into their vassals. Platforms like Grubhub, DoorDash, and Uber Eats charge restaurants with fees of up to 30 percent of the order price; but because the apps control access to the consumer seeking food delivery, restaurants have no choice but to pay.[57] Amazon exacts an array of fees—informational as well as monetary—from sellers in its marketplace, fees they can't avoid given Amazon's dominance of online retail sales. Describing Amazon as a "cloud fief," Yanis Varoufakis announces, "Enter amazon.com and you have exited capitalism."[58]

The historic process of separation that fragmented the pre-capitalist originary unity continues as middlemen, platforms, and intermediaries insert themselves into exchange relations, disrupt markets, and destroy sectors. Insertion, the creation of new dependencies based on monopoly power, doesn't come cheap. Domination costs billions, billions raised through venture capital and private equity, accumulations of wealth that increase through destructive rather than productive investment. Uber's strategy of using enormous amounts of capital to incentivize drivers and subsidize riders until the company has established itself in a city and can then start upping its fees and ride costs isn't unique. In the 2010s, it was practically gospel in Silicon Valley that the strategy for success was *lightning growth* or *blitzscaling*, a strategy that prioritizes market share over profit. According to Reid Hoffman, the cofounder of LinkedIn who coined the term, blitzscaling "involves purposefully and intentionally doing things that don't make sense according to traditional business thinking."[59]

WeWork is another example of a company that pursued this blitzscaling, this time in the office rental sector. WeWork's plan was to conquer market share as fast as it could. Armed with billions in investment capital from Japan's SoftBank Vision Fund, WeWork attempted to dominate markets in office space all over the world, using hoards of cash to destroy or purchase competitors, paying out huge incentives to early renters, and so on. WeWork's steps toward an initial public offering (IPO) in 2019 failed. SoftBank lost about 90 percent of its investment. WeWork finally declared bankruptcy in 2023.

What makes blitzscaling appear as a feasible strategy is the enormous amount of venture capital seeking outsized gains, especially the kind of gains that can accrue from a successful IPO. Billions in capital are funneled into a company so that it can destroy all potential competitors rather than having to compete with them directly through efficiency improvements. Once competitors are eliminated, and regulations and unions entirely circumvented, the victor can increase the squeeze on workers and customers alike. The laws of motion at work here are not capital's imperatives of profit maximization and competition in a market. Capital is a weapon of conquest and destruction.

Neoliberalism turns into neofeudalism because it destroys a particular set of state "fetters" or constraints on markets— employee safety nets, corporate taxation, and social welfare provisions. The enormous stores of wealth that neoliberal policies enable to accumulate in the hands of the few exert a political and economic power that protects the holders of wealth while intensifying the immiseration of almost everyone else. Wealth holders seeking high returns rely on speculative finance, hedge funds, private equity, venture capital, and the like to sniff out and chase after high-risk, high-reward pursuits of the kind favored in Silicon Valley. With goals of disruption and conquest, they throw this capital into destructive platforms that insert themselves into exchange relations rather than investing in production. Production isn't likely to generate significant profits, but platforms that can make themselves indispensable to market access, that can extract fees in novel ways, are more promising. The increase in precarity and anxiety, as well as the broader patterns associated with privatization, austerity, and the decline of the middle class, create a base of consumers grateful for price breaks and a supply of labor looking for work. Dependent on the market for access to our means of subsistence, we become dependent on the platform for access to the market. If we are to work, the platform gets its cut. If we are to consume, the platform gets its cut. At first it may seem that the price is just information. But it will increase. It does increase.

Neofeudalism results from the ongoing process of separation as it produces new social property relations, new intermediaries, new dependencies, and new laws of motion. It is not a "going back" to historical feudalism but a reflexivization such that capitalist processes long directed outward through colonialism and imperialism turn in on themselves. With production disconnected from accumulation, wealth is used as a weapon of conquest and destruction. Its hoarders and wielders are the new lords, the rest of us dependent, proletarianized serfs and servants. That we are proletarianized means that we continue to be dependent on the market for access to our means of life. Yet we have also been separated from the market and in that separation come under a double dependence, a dependence on intermediaries that will themselves provide us with market access—for a fee. The coercive force of the market is redoubled as an inescapable bondage to predators extracting rents, fees, life, and blood.

Despite the expression made popular by Slavoj Žižek and Mark Fisher that it's easier to imagine the end of the world than the end of capitalism, it's actually not true that we can't imagine the end of capitalism. Popular culture is filled with non-capitalist and post-capitalist worlds. What we have a hard time imagining is how it ends, how we get there, what the path from here to there looks like. The challenge comes not with thinking about capitalism as "over" but with seeing the various tendencies within capitalism, with figuring out what it is becoming.

Marx and Lenin understood capitalism as overlapping with and relying on preceding forms. Capitalism puts these preceding forms to use, subjects them to its logic, and often—but not always—changes them. A similar overlapping accompanies

capitalism's becoming neofeudal. The coincidence of employee/
independent contractor in platform labor marks this overlap.
Likewise, that market dependence remains a dominant feature
of life for the majority—a feature that endeavors organized as
"mutual aid" and urban gardening try to address—does not
mean that this is the same market dependence as that of the
so-called free worker. It's now a dependence into which intermediaries insert themselves. Rather than being thrown onto
the market, like the feudal retainers thrown out of the lords'
retinues, workers are separated from the labor market. They
can access it only if they pay tribute to the platforms controlling this access.

Harry Harootunian rightly criticizes Western Marxism for
its attachment to an image of an achieved capitalist society in
the West.[60] Dramatizing the contrast between backward and
advanced or developed, that image of achieved capitalist society made seeing the imbrications of backward and advanced
difficult for some Western Marxists. They failed to grasp how
advance itself creates decline, how production is destruction,
how prosperity for some is brought at the price of others.
Walter Rodney makes a similar argument in his classic *How
Europe Underdeveloped Africa*. The image of achieved capitalist society tricks us into thinking that there is only one
backwardness, and it's in the European past, a past falsely
universalized in developmentalist fictions, neither a present
cosynchronous with the achieved capitalist society nor a future
being ushered in. The neofeudal hypothesis aims to shatter
any remnants of that image.

2

Forward Can Be Backward: On Transition and Temporality

Capital is turning into something that is no longer capitalist, where holders of wealth are compelled to follow different laws of motion, not competition, reinvestment, and improvement but predation, hoarding, and destruction. Capital is becoming neofeudal. That it's *becoming* means that we can't say we are in a completely new period; it's not dead yet. We're in a period of transition, and transition can last a long, long time. The challenge is understanding transition while we're in it and aren't sure where we're going.

Marxists have long grappled with the question of transition. Whether debating the transition from feudalism to capitalism or considering how capitalism creates the opening for communism, Marxists generally approach the question as a problem of fundamental systemic change.[1] How is social, political, and economic transformation possible? How does one kind of society and mode of production become another one? The question may be posed as the issue of stages of historical development and periods of revolutionary struggle, the determining dynamic of technological innovation, the alternative of reform or revolution, the role of the dictatorship of the proletariat, or even the classic political-theory dilemma of how people who have grown up in chains might build a free society. How do we get from oppression to freedom?

McKenzie Wark's provocative question, "What if we're not in capitalism anymore but something worse?" takes aim at stagist assumptions fettering left accounts of transition. Too many Marxists seem to assume a linear progression from slavery to feudalism, to capitalism, to socialism, and toward communism. Since socialism has yet to be built, they conclude that we must still be in capitalism. Blinkered by this underlying stagism, left analyses remain unable to theorize the present. They're trapped in the premise that just as the bourgeoisie defeated the feudal lords, so must the industrial proletariat defeat the bourgeoisie, and that capitalism will persist until it does. But what happens when the working class has lost? If capital is a relation, wouldn't that loss change capitalism into something else? The presumptions of stagist Marxism prevent the question from even being posed. Something like neofeudalism would be impossible from the outset, a going backward when history moves only forward.

Fortunately, the Marxist tradition has a richer, more complex approach to time and history than the old developmentalist story of linear stages.[2] This tradition is important for the neofeudal hypothesis because it demonstrates how labor forms, laws of motion, modes of production, and accumulation strategies are never as pure as we imagine. The complex temporalities interwoven throughout Marxist theory allow for overlap and incompleteness, processes associated with earlier modes of production coinciding with those of later modes.[3] Reversals and retrogressions subvert presumptions of straightforward march to a certain future. Development is uneven, inextricable from de-development. Features associated with one period or category slide into those of the period left behind or entered into. Attending to these complex temporalities lets us theorize transition without presupposing linear stages. We can see combinations of old and new forms and dynamics, getting a better grasp of the alternatives available for contestation. We can identify tendencies, without positing a certain and inevitable historical telos. And we can recognize even in accounts presuming an inevitable communism guidance for analyzing what went wrong. The complex temporalities of transitions to capitalism can tell us about transitions out of it, whether in the gloomy direction of neofeudalism or something more emancipatory and egalitarian.

When we combine unevenness with the multi-directionality of transition, with the fact that things can get worse, we realize the unavoidability of politics: without power we will lose. Our enemies will fight back. Counterrevolution is real. Acknowledging this should not engender hopelessness and defeatism. It should remind us that communists fight because we must: we have a world to win.

Neither linear nor stagist

Capitalist production has always coexisted with prior modes of production, as well as with non-bourgeois and non-capitalist ideologies and practices such as feudal political and legal forms. Considering the United States, Marx underscores how slavery, ostensibly a past economic form, was indispensable to the capitalistic production of cotton for the world market, compounding "civilized" with "barbaric" horror (and thereby undercutting the conceits of the so-called civilized).[4] Marx's political writing expresses a similar sense of the weight of the "traditions of dead generations." In "The Eighteenth Brumaire of Louis Bonaparte," he famously says that "men make their own history, but they do not make it just as they please; they do not make it under circumstances chosen by themselves, but under circumstances directly encountered, given and transmitted from the past."[5] Elements from the past persist in the present; existing in the present, they are features of the present impacting human action. The present doesn't erase the past. Sometimes it even preserves it.

Ostensibly obsolete economic forms can reappear. In a set of letters from December 1882, Engels writes to Marx that he is glad that they "proceed in agreement" regarding the reappearance of serfdom in the fifteenth and sixteenth centuries after it had virtually disappeared in Europe in the thirteenth and fourteenth centuries. Engels criticizes the historian Georg Ludwig von Maurer (whose work he had been studying) for presuming "steady progress to better things" since the Middle Ages.[6] Although it's common to present Marxism as a theory of history's march from slavery, through feudalism, to capitalism, socialism, and onward to communism, Marx and Engels resist reduction to a linear, progressive theory of historical change. Especially in their later writing, capital does not overthrow feudalism, bursting loose from its fetters and establishing itself once and for all. Transition is extended, complex, uncertain, and reversible.

Lenin too resists reduction to linear history. His political moves in this regard are well known: his insistence that the Bolsheviks prepare for—and lead—a socialist revolution in a country where capitalism had barely developed; his introduction of capitalism (the New Economic Policy) as a necessary tactical retreat from the project of building socialism following the economic devastation of civil war. The premise of Lenin's theory of the state in the transition to communism is the endurance of bourgeois forms during the socialist phase: "remnants of the old, surviving in the new, confront us in life at every step, both in nature and in society."[7] His theory of imperialism highlights reversal: capitalism became capitalist imperialism "when certain of its fundamental characteristics began to change into their opposites."[8] No linearity here.

Lenin's analysis of the emergence of capitalism in Russia likewise evinces an understanding of transition as open, complex, and honeycombed with contradictory forms and tendencies. He details the differentiation among the Russian peasantry—upper, middle, and poor peasants; various forms of ownership, labor extraction, and payment (including wage labor); the persistence of the coercive practices associated with serfdom after its official abolition in 1861. Lenin pays particular attention to the transition to capitalist agriculture from the corvée (*barshchina*) form of agricultural labor. The corvée system relied on peasants providing lords with labor services: peasants held land and tools but depended on access to land that remained in the lords' possession, land such as watering places, woods, and meadows. In principle, peasants agreed to work for the landlords in exchange for rights of access; in practice, they were often directly coerced. The capitalist agricultural system relied on waged workers. Whether hired seasonally or as day laborers, these peasant workers didn't use their own tools, and they had to work for hire (sell their labor power) because they had no land (lacked means of subsistence). Important to Lenin is less the distinction between the corvée and capitalist forms of agricultural labor than their coexistence during the transition to capitalism. The combination of dissimilar systems, he tells us, "leads in practice to a whole number of most profound and complicated conflicts and contradictions."[9] Lenin continues: "Life creates forms that unite in themselves with remarkable gradualness systems of economy whose basic features constitute opposites. It becomes impossible to say where 'labor-service' ends and where 'capitalism' begins."

Rosa Luxemburg argues that capital accumulation depends on "non-capitalist social strata and forms of social organization."[10] Marx had already emphasized the "primitive accumulation" at capital's origins, drawing out the violence of colonialism as well as domestic processes whereby producers were separated from the means of production. Luxemburg highlights capital's ongoing dependence on an outside that it expropriates through violent means, employing "force as a permanent weapon."[11] While Luxemburg attends to slavery and serfdom, her prime example is European colonial expansion, carried out "by a relentless battle of capital against the social and economic ties of the natives, who are also forcibly robbed of their means of production and labor power."[12] She looks closely at French colonialism in Algeria, British colonialism in India, China, and South Africa, and the forced removal and killing off of Indigenous people in the westward expansion of the United States. In all, the lesson is the same: the capitalist economy develops in and depends on a non-capitalist outside that it violently subdues—and this very process of subjugation intensifies capital's imperialist, lawless violence by rendering ever scarcer the outside on which capital depends.[13]

Focusing on colonialism in Africa, Walter Rodney deepens Luxemburg's argument. Capital doesn't simply depend on a non-capitalist or pre-capitalist outside that could potentially enter into the world trading system and eventually catch up. Capital, particularly in its imperialist phase, actively under-develops huge parts of the world. What looks like forward movement, development from one angle is exploitation, oppression, and underdevelopment from another. Countries aren't simply at different stages along a path heading in one direction. Africa's integration into the capitalist world economy is precisely what renders it exploited and dependent. Rodney is writing in the early 1970s, a time when "the capitalist epoch is not quite over."[14] He observes that "those who live at a particular point in time often fail to see that their way of life is in the process of transformation and elimination."[15] Rodney thinks that the capitalist system is "rapidly expiring" in the wake of fifty years of socialist success. Yet he warns that "modes of production cannot simply be viewed as a question of successive stages."[16] Not only has socialism not replaced capitalism, but capitalist exploitation of underdeveloped countries is expanding and intensifying their underdevelopment. Multiple political and economic forms coexist, but hardly peacefully.

René Zavaleta Mercado shows how Spanish colonialism created a "deeply ingrained seigneurial-servile culture" in

Bolivia.[17] He considers the ostensible paradox of a "formally capitalist sector" in an environment that was not capitalist.[18] The silver mines of Potosí that made European capital possible didn't make that region capitalist. They produced for a world market, but not capitalistically. The mines' owners weren't capitalists in any strong sense. Their mentality was feudal, seigneurial, a mentality that became permanently inscribed in the Bolivian oligarchy. Instead of reinvesting the surplus the mines generated in improvements, the owners purchased massive amounts of land and built extravagant palaces. Labor relations weren't capitalist either. The vast majority of workers were Indigenous people directly conscripted into forced labor (the infamous *mita*) and paid not in wages but in goods produced on the owners' lands. Zavaleta writes, "It is reasonable to maintain that, from the very moment the Spaniards set foot on these lands, the most consistent precapitalist element is the theft of labor power."[19] The second most consistent is the theft of land. By the beginning of the twentieth century, over 60 percent of the land in Bolivia was held by less than 10 percent of the people—a dramatic change from the middle of the nineteenth century, when 90 percent of the land was still owned by peasants. The legally enacted expropriation of Indigenous land led to something like a second serfdom (in contrast to the expropriation of the English enclosure movement associated with the emergence of capitalism).[20] Formerly free workers were now servile workers bound to the land.

Zavaleta notes the fundamental difference between European feudalism and Bolivia's seigneurial system: the Bolivian system was "constructed in the encounter with the Indian."[21] He explains (employing Hegel): "Where there is no Indian, there is no lord."[22] Racial difference functioned as a crucial element of subjugation: society is founded on inequality, endless graduated hierarchies ensuring "that there is always someone lower in rank."[23] The seigneurial aspect of the system also manifests in the fact that "there is no lord without land."[24] Land conferred a title imagined to bestow a nobility akin to that of Spanish lords to those who were not Spanish lords but who fetishized and fantasized their position. Land was symbolic and reproductive, feudal rather than capitalist. Holding the land had a mystical quality never fully adequate to the task of mitigating the racial uncertainty of the landowning class.

One last figure in the Marxist tradition of rejecting linear stages and recognizing a complex temporality of overlaps and reversals is Louis Althusser. In the posthumously published *Philosophy of the Encounter*, he asks:

> What proves the feudal mode of production declines and decays, then eventually disappears? It was not until 1850–70 that capitalism established itself firmly in France. Above all, given that the bourgeoisie is said to be the product of the feudal mode of production, what proves that it was not a class of the feudal mode of production, and a sign of the reinforcement rather than the decay of this model?[25]

Althusser doesn't pursue this line. Rather than considering a dialectic of decay and reinforcement or of classes functioning on behalf of seemingly opposed modes of production, he is interested in opening up the aleatory, in viewing transition as a matter of chance encounters that may or may not take hold. His skepticism regarding feudalism's mythical decay is well-founded. Yet Althusser's conceptualization of modes of production as structures that impose their unity on a series of elements obscures the combinations and interactions of modes of production. It's as if he introduces the question of complex temporalities, of continuities and reinforcements that undermine and support, only to push it aside. As chance overrides decay, the opportunity to consider the overlaps of forms and logics is closed off in favor of a clear delineation of structures: feudalism with its structure of dependence and capitalism with its structure of exploitation.[26] At a minimum one might want to ask about forms of dependence on exploitation and the exploitation of dependence. Different modes of production can coexist, contributing to the reproduction of processes and relations that they transform.

Theorizing contemporaneity

Historians Jairus Banaji and Harry Harootunian give theoretical expression to the combinations and reversals of economic forms and logics that the Marxist tradition has long acknowledged. Emphasizing agrarian capitalism and the provincialism of Western Marxism, respectively, Banaji and Harootunian draw out the multiple, differentiated, and uneven trajectories of capitalist development. Their analyses highlight concepts useful for navigating complex temporalities and theorizing transition without presuming that history unfolds along a determined path of linear stages.

Banaji emphasizes the distinction between relations of production and forms of exploitation.[27] He employs this distinction—which he finds in the Marxist tradition—in a critique of the Marxist tradition, from "vulgar Marxism" in the twenties and thirties, through midcentury debates over the transition from feudalism to capitalism, to the 1970s debate between Ernesto Laclau and André Gunder Frank over underdevelopment in Latin America. Most significant for my discussion is Banaji's emphasis on laws of motion. Much like Ellen Meiksins Wood, Banaji takes the view that modes of production cannot be defined in terms of specific labor processes. The same labor processes can be found in different modes of production. Commodity production appears in feudalism; factory owners sometimes use serf labor; slave plantations generate surplus value for capitalists. An enormous array of labor forms sustains feudal enterprise, not just serfs but also part-time workers, free tenants, day laborers, and legally enslaved domestic workers.[28] Capitalism likewise relies on coerced, unwaged, and unfree labor. Rather than being characterized by their mechanisms of surplus labor extraction, modes of production are differentiated by their underlying dynamics, their specific laws of motion. Whereas capitalist production is driven by the imperative of accumulation (with its accompanying compulsions to compete and improve), the driver of feudal production is the consumption needs of lords. So even as free labor and commodity production appear under feudalism—and, indeed, Banaji argues that feudalism "crystalized" as "commodity feudalism"—what matters are the laws of motion behind the coercive shape that feudalism takes: generating the cash needed to fund the lords' consumption.

Banaji draws out the repercussions of this emphasis on laws of motion for understanding colonialism. Arguing that the colonization of Latin America "was a *feudal* colonization, a response to the crisis of feudal profitability which all the land-owning classes of Europe were facing down to the latter part of the sixteenth century," he rejects the dominant assumption in the Laclau-Frank debate—namely, that colonization was driven by the imperative of capital accumulation.[29] Laclau and Frank take for granted the laws of motion that an earlier generation of Marxists knew had to be discovered underneath empirical appearances. Converting capitalism's "points of arrival into points of departure," they fail to recognize how similar forms had radically different laws of motion.[30] In Latin America and parts of South Asia, feudal estates produced commodities for national and international markets (as we've already seen in Zavaleta). In the West Indies, most of Africa, and much of Asia, capitalist firms relied on "archaic ('pre-capitalist') modes of labor-organization and generally stagnant levels of technique."[31] While Marx recognized these "inter-mediate, hybrid forms," Banaji points out that they've persisted longer than the large-scale production typically associated with capitalism.[32] A one-sided emphasis on forms of exploitation, coupled with the erasure of feudal laws of motion under the assumption of specifically capitalist motivation, blocks their differences from view, misrepresenting and misunderstanding each.

Harootunian emphasizes formal subsumption. As he explains, Marx's concept of formal subsumption refers "to the encounter of capitalism and received practices at hand." Labor practices "belonging to a prior mode of production" are resituated "alongside and within newer capitalist demands to create value."[33] Temporal unevenness thus occupies the heart of Marx's theory of capital accumulation. Neither a remnant nor an outside, pre-capitalist or non-capitalist relations of exploitation are directly incorporated in capitalist production in the operation of formal subsumption.[34] The old is preserved as a precondition of the new. Whereas many commentators view real subsumption as the point when capitalism is fully established, since this is when capital transforms labor processes in order to generate surplus value, Harootunian argues that for Marx formal subsumption is the key to capitalist development. Capital always appropriates what it finds on hand, "subjugating older practices and institutions" to its logic.[35] Western Marxism, however, has fixated on real subsumption: the commodification of everything, domination of the value form, and triumph of capital. The resulting "image of achieved capitalist society in the West" presumes a flattening uniformity, not only obscuring historical difference but also disavowing capital's reliance on the unevenness it produces.[36]

Harootunian endeavors to deprovincialize Marx by showing how thinkers beyond the industrial capitalist core use and develop Marxist categories to theorize unevenness. To this end, he reads José Carlos Mariátegui's layered account of the unresolved land question in Peru. Mariátegui emphasizes not just the colonial implantation of feudalism but also its reliance on extermination, slavery, and extraction as well as its mutation into a persistent semi-feudalism. Envisioning strata of economic forms one on top of the other, he sees in Indigenous communities enduring traces of an Incan communism and cooperative tradition. Harootunian writes:

> Mariátegui demonstrated how the semifeudal mutation represented both the sign of formal subsumption and the society it wrought into a permanent transition caught in the constant collision of pasts in presents that are never completed but always left open; not a society distinguished by a polarization of opposites and the successful overcoming of one by the other, nor the grand transition from a noncommodity community—feudalism—or any comparable tributary system to market society or one faithful to exchange.[37]

Formal subsumption's retaining of the past renders transition an open question, a process never fully complete. The past isn't left behind but perpetually part of an ongoing transition.

Taking up debates over the development of capitalism in China and Japan, Harootunian considers opposing interpretations of feudalism: Wang Yanan's charge that enduring feudalism provided a barrier to capitalist development in China and Uno Kōzō's argument that feudal residues benefited Japan's capitalism.[38] While critical of Wang's reliance on a stagist Marxism that smooths over a more astute treatment of unevenness, Harootunian commends Wang's insight into the alignment of feudal structure and imperialism as a clear statement of the logic of formal subsumption. The very elements of the traditional economy that foreign capital was restructuring, in other words, that were being put to use in capitalist production, also operated as constraints on capitalist development. An uneven history bound together primitive and capitalist accumulation, freezing them in place.[39] Uno's analysis of development in Japan also focuses on the interplay of feudal and capitalist elements, from the ways that specific forms interact with and change each other, to the persistence of feudal sentiments even after the demise of feudal social relations (an argument akin to Zavaleta's). Far from a feature specific to Japan, the persistence of elements from the past into the present is a general feature of capitalism everywhere, the basic dynamic of formal subsumption where capital takes what it finds.

Banaji's and Harootunian's insights into the dynamics of complex temporalities demonstrate ways of approaching transition without falling into stagism and determinism. That forms associated with one period exist in another doesn't mean they function in the same way or follow the same laws of motion they once did. Capital embraces, absorbs, and capitalizes on feudal processes and relations. Formal subsumption is the bringing of old forms under a new logic. Feudal processes and relations may be fetters on or agents of capitalist development. Transition isn't a clean break. The persistence of past elements complicates clear descriptions of the present and holds the future in suspense.

Transition or communism?

The complex temporalities disrupting stagist accounts of the transition from feudalism to capitalism reappear in theorizations of the transition from capitalism to communism. A paradox persists at the core of Marxist thought: communism builds from capitalism, is made possible by capitalism, and is its negation, a radical break from all that exists. Lenin finds the resolution of the paradox in the state, more specifically, in the dictatorship of the proletariat as a transitional state form.[40] The emancipation of the proletariat involves more than winning political power. It requires the proletariat's active exercise

of power with the goal of building communism. Bourgeois resistance has to be suppressed. Classes have to dissolve. The people
have to develop new habits and capacities. The movement from
capitalism to communism is a transition. "Dictatorship of the
proletariat" names the political form of that transition: a state
that aims at its own dissolution.

Étienne Balibar takes up Lenin's discussion of the dictatorship of the proletariat in the context of debates in the French
Communist Party (PCF) in the 1970s. Like other communist
parties in Western Europe, the PCF abandoned the dictatorship of the proletariat in favor of the so-called democratic
road to socialism. Against this "Eurocommunist" position,
Balibar argues that there isn't a transition *to* socialism. Socialism is not a transitional mode of production between capitalism
and communism. Socialism is a transitional *period* within capitalism. It denotes a time when there are classes and class
conflict, multiple contradictory interests, and the persistence
of the bourgeois legal form. The dictatorship of the proletariat
isn't an alternative to socialism; it is socialism.[41] Both name
the period of transition from capitalism to communism.
Reformist Eurocommunists failed to understand this.

Balibar emphasizes that the dictatorship of the proletariat
is necessarily more than the form of a state that aims at its
own dissolution. It is also *"the reality of an historical tendency."*[42] Communism develops out of the contradictions of
capitalism—the socialization of production and the class
struggle through which the proletariat learns to organize itself
and replace competition with solidarity. These two forms in
which communism tendentially appears under capitalism
oppose each other, only coming together with the proletariat's
revolutionary seizure of power. Balibar writes: "History has
shown that the conditions for such a revolution are only produced by capitalism when it has arrived at the stage of
imperialism, and unevenly from country to country, though
the movement is globally irreversible (which does not mean

that it is irreversible in any particular case)."[43] Imperialism is the stage when revolution against capitalism becomes not just possible but inevitable.

Balibar's assumption of unidirectional movement has not been borne out. From the fragmentation of production associated with neoliberal globalization to the defeats suffered by the working class and the communist movement, the fragility of socialist victories is impossible to deny. Nevertheless, his insight into the simultaneous and contradictory development of imperialism and the dictatorship of the proletariat is indispensable. Balibar reminds us not only of the unevenness inextricable from imperialism but also of the fact that imperialism is a stage of capitalism. The dictatorship of the proletariat is the political form through which the proletariat wages class struggle within this stage.

At the time Balibar was writing, much of the communist movement emphasized the opposition between socialism and imperialism. The assumption was that they were two utterly separate and completely opposed camps. Balibar rejects this thesis, arguing for their mutual imbrication. Neither form is pure; they interact with and influence each other. He explains:

> The notion of the "two worlds" places Communists in an impossible position: the socialist world represents "the future," the imperialist world represents "the past"; between this past and this future there can by definition be no interdependence, no interaction, simply the tenuous thread of a moment of transition, all the more difficult to grasp because it is still to come, and yet has already taken place.[44]

The presumption of two separate worlds makes it theoretically impossible for socialism to imagine revolutions occurring within imperialism. It prevents analysis of conflicts within the socialist bloc and of the influence of capital on socialist countries. In contrast, imperialism understood temporally, as an epoch, places socialist development within this period or stage. Socialism influences and is influenced by imperialism, the time of its development.

As is well known, Lenin defines imperialism as a stage of capitalism characterized by five basic features: monopolies, finance capital, export of capital rather than the export of commodities, international associations of monopoly capital, and the division of the world among the largest capitalist powers.[45] Uneven development and colonial exploitation—combinations of different labor processes, different forms of exploitation, different modes of production—are thus quintessential elements of imperialism. Placing socialism within the imperialist epoch, Balibar recognizes this intermeshing. Yet in his effort to refute the idea that socialism is a distinct mode of production, he gives a misleading presentation of capitalism.[46] He presents capital as the absolute separation of the laborer from the means of production despite the fact that formal subsumption allows for continued connection. He centers the buying and selling of labor power even as wage labor is found in non-capitalist labor arrangements. He omits capital's laws of motion, which would help make sense of the combinations of different labor processes. He says that "all law, from the beginning of capitalism onwards, is bourgeois," which neglects the continuation of feudal legal forms as well as the common law tradition.[47] And, most significant, he presumes temporal progress and linearity, imposing historical direction on top of his assumption of stages.

The relation between labor and capital, Balibar writes, is the "*last possible* relation of exploitation in history: once having arrived there, you can neither return to former modes of exploitation—in which the laborer enjoys a certain form of possession of his means of production and a certain individual control over their use—nor go forward to a 'new' mode of exploitation."[48] Balibar echoes Marx here.[49] Today such claims of finality and irreversibility aren't compelling. Particularly in the wake of the defeat of the workers' movement at the end of the twentieth century and the rise of new forms of servitude and exploitation in the twenty-first, former Marxist certainties have lost the power to convince. Uber drivers, for example, enjoy "a certain form of possession" of their means of production and a "certain individual control over their use"—and this very enjoyment is the mechanism through which capital is able to escape the constraints put on it by victories in working-class struggle. Entire countries can win independence, overthrowing their colonial oppressors, only to find themselves bound to capitalist financial institutions, corporate investments, and international trade agreements they have no choice but to sign. The very fact that socialism denotes a form of struggle and transition occurring during the imperialist era, and that during that era socialism and imperialism affect and transform each other, means there are no guarantees.

Antonio Negri agrees with Balibar that socialism is a stage of capitalism. Where he disagrees is whether it can be understood as a transitional stage in the development of communism. Negri claims that "communism is in no case a product of capitalist development, it is its radical inversion."[50] Rather than theorizing the transition to communism, Negri replaces transition with communism. Communism is the actual movement that inverts and negates capital.

Negri makes this claim in the context of a close reading of the *Grundrisse* as a theory of revolutionary subjectivity. His argument depends on real subsumption. The development of machinery transforms labor processes for the benefit of capital. The productive knowledge and skills of workers are absorbed into machines—that is, fixed capital. At the same time, because capital necessarily exceeds use, is utterly indifferent to any specific form of use value, machinery can't appear as the most adequate form of capital. That form is circulating capital, not fixed capital. Productive capital thus involves the labor process and circulation, capital's social movement. Negri writes: "Real subsumption of labor can't but be (in the same moment) real subsumption of society."[51] Just as machinery transforms the labor process, so does circulation transform society.

Capital's subsumption of society has repercussions for the theory of value. Wealth creation depends less on labor time and more on the application of science and technology to production. This creates contradictions: on the one hand, capital posits labor time as the measure and source of wealth; on the other, machinery reduces necessary labor time. With the widespread adoption of machinery, capital diminishes necessary labor time in order to increase surplus labor time, making surplus labor time a condition for necessary labor time. The very machinery that should make it possible for workers to have more free time ends up locking them into longer hours because of its capitalist form. In *Factory of Strategy*, Negri summarizes the analysis:

> The law of value, which ought to represent the rationality of exploitation (and the scientific key to its interpretation), must lose its rationalizing and legitimating plausibility within the very development of the capitalist mode of production. Marx shows how the demise of the function of the law of value simultaneously corresponds (as cause and effect) to the enormous and formidable growth of the productive, free, and innovative potential of the proletariat.[52]

Under conditions of real subsumption, the form of the law of value is capitalist command. Abolishing, or negating, this power of command is communism.

Real subsumption's undoing of the theory of value makes socialism impossible. As a stage where each is compensated in accordance with their work, socialism presumes that there is some kind of rational quantitative measure capable of ensuring a fair distribution. Large-scale industry's collective worker eliminates the possibility of such a measurement. Distribution, or redistribution, can be determined only on the basis of political criteria (which demonstrates the pointlessness of re-rationalizing the capitalist law of value). Since capitalism has already undermined the function of the law of value, what is necessary is destroying "every form of command immediately" and liberating "class from labor."[53] The abolition of command, and along with it the machinery and technology comprising capitalist command's material structure, thereby replaces transition with communism: the liberation of living labor. As Negri rather enigmatically puts it, "it is not the transition that reveals itself (and eliminates itself) in the form of communism, but rather it is communism that takes the form of the transition."[54] Communism is the process through which working-class subjectivity emerges within and in violent antagonism to capital.

That Negri's argument is premised on real subsumption implies that formal subsumption isn't sufficiently capitalist for communist movement: it's the widespread adoption of machinery, the development of industry on a large scale, that leads to the breakdown of the law of value and its transformation into nothing but capitalist command. A "completed" (to use Harootunian's term) capitalism therefore appears to be necessary for communist movement. If this is the case, communism becomes a project of the West or the North, of fully industrialized countries, their de-developed peripheries not only left behind but perpetually pushed behind and away from communist possibilities. The colonized or formerly colonized remain outside a communist future, communism unavailable as a name for their liberation. Paradoxically, or perhaps ironically given Negri's justified distance from Eurocommunism, communism appears as the self-consciousness strictly of the

European working class rather than as the orientation and victory of worker and peasant struggles in Russia and China. If Luxemburg is correct regarding capital's dependence on an outside, or if Lenin is correct regarding imperialism as an epoch of the territorial division of the world into colonial possessions, then communism seems literally unreachable, not simply antagonistic to capital but so separate from it as to be unable to touch it. Working-class subjectivity emerges as an autonomous process of self-valorization, in and as separation from capital, without admixture, without imbrication, not unlike the two-world thesis Balibar correctly rejects.

The premise of real subsumption—unfortunately pervasive on the contemporary left, not least because of the influence of communization theorists—erases differentiation within capitalism. Remnants of the past that could be appropriate for communism—forms of communal belonging, say, or Indigenous practices of agroecological farming—disappear. Non-capitalist labor processes and their role in supporting as well as hindering the development of capitalism fall from view. Layers of history are flattened out into a smooth, uniform present. For all Negri's insistence on overthrowing "all kinds of necessity and determinism attributed to the process of transition," he sneaks them in through the back door of real subsumption.[55] Not only do we know where we are going, communism is already here.

But what if it's not? Negri's erasure of multiple temporalities and his assumption of direction—communism as what opposes and follows capitalism—preclude consideration of what happens if workers lose, capital triumphs, and the whole apparatus of exploitation and command continues churning along. Fortunately, his analysis suggests ways to understand the repercussions of working-class defeat, even as he takes the perspective of workers' victory. Negri's account of the change from surplus value to capitalist command highlights the way the law of value becomes implausible within capitalism.

Capital's own processes erode it, disconnecting wage labor from any materially productive economic basis. Wages and salaries are determined politically, linked to the maintenance of class structure. Repercussions of this shift to command appear in the gross inequalities in pay between executives and employees, between upper management and lower-tier workers, between platform billionaires and the sector of servants. The limits to the heights and depths of compensation are political, dependent on power: Are the holders of wealth able to command tax cuts? Are those who sell their labor power to survive able to unionize? Do interest rates encourage debt, and how do these debts contribute to class formation (by allowing, say, purchasers of debt to increase their wealth while debtors themselves become virtual prisoners perpetually bound to endless repayment)?

Even more significant are the limits that investment in fixed capital come up against. Widespread adoption of machinery intensifies competition and diminishes returns. As Robert Brenner and Aaron Benanav argue, overcapacity in world markets for manufactured goods has driven global deindustrialization and stagnation.[56] An effect has been the shedding of jobs in industry and the dramatic increase in jobs in services. Nonstandard and informal employment has expanded, especially in the Global South, as workers cobble together income from different forms of labor service. From one angle, self-employment looks like self-exploitation; from another it appears as generalized servitude, dependence on the consumption habits of service-seekers with disposable income. The fragmentation and disintegration of labor in the context of deindustrialization suggests that contra Negri, capitalist development is clearly reversible and dependent on multiple forms of non-capitalist labor. Premising analyses of capital on real subsumption today misses the opportunity to see the struggles linked to fragmenting and declining capitalism as locations of its weakness, its inability to secure its own conditions.

Correlative to declining economic growth and the steady rise in services has been hoarding and rentierism. Capital accumulation occurs more from intellectual property, patents, and fees than from the production of goods, from rent rather than profit. Corporations don't invest their proceeds; they buy back stocks and increase executive compensation, eating their profits in old seigneurial style. Capital's laws of motion turn into their opposites as the drive to accumulate incentivizes plunder and hoarding rather than investment and improvement.

Balibar observes that periods of transition are "characterized by the *coexistence* of several modes of production."[57] Extracted from the assumption that we know what we are transitioning to, his insight suggests that our present may not be accurately described simply as capitalist. It may in fact be becoming something else, something where feudal dynamics emerge out of capitalist incentives. Coexistence points to the ways that the same labor processes may follow different laws of motion: service labor may be reproductive but not productive, more likely remunerated out of consumption funds than consumed as part of production. In the same vein, when finance operates destructively, does it even make sense to think of it as capitalist? Leveraged buyouts enable financiers to take over companies, saddle them with debt, and sell off their components. Start-ups like WeWork and Uber rely on massive infusions of private equity to "disrupt" entire sectors. Complex debt instruments led to over $7 trillion of losses in the 2008 financial crisis. The "logic" here is feudal: pillage and plunder.

Balibar's emphasis on imperialism as a stage of capitalism reminds us of the constitutive unevenness of global capital. The world isn't smooth or flat. It comprises losers and winners, poor and rich, exploited and exploiter. Capital relies on this unevenness, on non-capitalist modes of production, labor processes, and forms of exploitation. Such reliance indicates points of weakness. Whether these weaknesses will support or undermine capital, whether they can be mobilized on behalf of emancipation or commandeered for something worse depends on political struggle.

3

Neofeudalism's Basic Features

Neofeudalism isn't a concept reliant on a detailed history of actually existing feudalism. As a vision of where capitalism is heading, it relies on contemporary analyses of law, social property relations, spatiality, and affect, on seeing how developments that have previously been considered separate are in fact deeply interconnected. This chapter describes the primary features of neofeudalism in terms of these four categories, highlighting parcellated sovereignty, new lords and serfs, hinterlandization, and catastrophic anxiety.

The chapter begins with a sketch of the changes in state form accompanying the neoliberal assault on the welfare state and enabling the political emergence of neofeudalism. The last forty years of neoliberalism have unraveled the sovereignty associated first with the monarchies of early European modernity and then with the people in bourgeois democracies. Almost as if history were running backward, sovereignty is becoming suzerainty. States exist as governments over people and territory, yet they lack the ability to act independently. Like so many oath-bound vassals, their range of movement is curtailed by myriad treaties and agreements, by the preferences of investors and asset holders, by the dominance of imperial powers, and by their own self-fragmentation. As the few have been able to exercise economic power as political power, the many have been pushed into servitude, unable to avoid ever-rising fees, fines, rents, and penalties. Not only have the people lost the fantasy of sovereignty; they've lost what little freedom popular struggle attained.

From sovereignty to suzerainty

Although always more complicated in actual practice, economic liberalism relied on the idea of free people in free markets. With a constitutional state securing rights to property and upholding fair contracts, the hardworking and resourceful could make their fortune and benefit society. Their productive investment would provide employment for the many, keeping workers in their place while rewarding the industrious. Relations in the factory may have been despotic, but the conceit of contract was that they were freely chosen. Society may have been competitive, even somewhat anarchic, but bourgeois constitutional law supplied the minimal conditions necessary for the self-government of free men. Even if it was never realized in practice, this was the story the liberal democratic state used to legitimate itself and the capitalist mode of production it protected.

The Fordist welfare state changes this story. The state might claim to be liberal and democratic, but its legitimacy doesn't stem from securing rights and liberties. It stems from its ability to maintain the conditions necessary for capital accumulation. As Antonio Negri argues, the welfare state socializes exploitation, exercising despotism throughout society on capital's behalf.[1] Society becomes a "social factory." Functioning as what Marx would call "an abstract capitalist," the state recognizes its dependence on the working class. The working class can't be eliminated; capital accumulation requires it. But the working class is dangerous, an ever-present threat to an always uncertain and risky future. From the perspective of capitalists, workers are the "party of catastrophe." The repercussion of the state's direct involvement in securing the reproduction of capitalism is that, as Negri puts it, "the settling of accounts with the party of catastrophe becomes a daily event."[2] The Fordist era presented the incorporation of the working class into the capitalist state in terms of class compromise, reformism, and the common good. The reality was that capital's becoming the state opened it to "contestation and contradiction." The state responds to the precarity of capital's position—to the difficulty of securing equilibrium—with force, repression, and violence. Economic problems are immediately political.

The struggles associated with this settling of accounts intensified during the revolutionary period of 1968. Women, workers, students, Black people, Brown people, colonized people, Indigenous people, people against war, people against sexual oppression, and people against the suffocating despotism of the social factory claimed the liberties promised by democracy. Capital responded with neoliberal globalization, paying for the restoration of capitalist power by surrendering features previously reserved to sovereignty. If sovereignty was the organized power of the people, if the concerns and interests of the working class could not be excluded from it, then sovereignty itself would have to go. It would have to be limited, shared, unraveled.

Neoliberalism was the ideological and policy apparatus for this unraveling. It undermined sovereignty, which in no way means that it eroded coercive state power. Finance capital subjected states to markets. Operating outside of the traditional structures of bourgeois representative government, the demands of investors and financiers decreased the political effectiveness of law and elections. Just as the state came to function as a collective capitalist in charge of the social factory under Fordism, so did it come to serve the needs of finance capital, reorganizing the global division of labor, appropriating profit, and extracting rent "from the production and reproduction of life and from the communication and circulation of value."[3]

Quinn Slobodian recounts the development of the neoliberal strategy of undermining the economic authority of the nation-state in the interest of advancing global trade. Threatened by the organized demands coming from the newly independent nations of the Global South for reparations, sovereignty over their own natural resources, stabilized commodity prices, and the regulation of transnational corporations, neoliberals in the 1970s sought to "circumvent the authority of national governments."[4] They advocated a multilevel approach to regulation, a competitive federalism that would enable capital to discipline governments while itself remaining immunized from democratic control. In the words of Hans Willgerodt, one of the neoliberals Slobodian studies, the new competitive federalism required the state to "share its sovereignty downward with federal structures and bind itself upward within an international legal community."[5] This global legal architecture fragments sovereignty. It's as if neoliberalism is the vanishing mediator that, intending to protect capitalism, creates the conditions for its demise, for its evolution into a form of accumulation and control that can no longer be understood in terms of a capitalist system separated between public and private, state and market, coercion and consent.

Neoliberalism's reformulation of power from transcendental state command to immanent global control does not expand the social factory to the global level. The logic and mechanisms of control aren't exercised from above; they're exercised across and through, unevenly and transversally. There isn't a centralized world power or one world government; there's a multilayered patchwork of crisscrossing agreements and treaties designed to benefit the powerful and to subject and contain the weak. Negri pinpoints the structural obstacle sovereignty encounters under neoliberalism as the "uncertain relationship between exceptionality and precariousness."[6] Exceptionality has lost the transcendental status attributed to it by Carl Schmitt, becoming immanent in the need for daily decisions "amid the precariousness of the juridical fabric." By moving to the global level, capital—or, more precisely, monopoly holders of assets and hoarders of wealth—frees itself from state-imposed constraints. Tax rates too high? Incorporate in the Cayman Islands. Burdened by high labor costs? Build or find a factory in an enterprise zone, maybe even one that subsidizes labor costs. Worried about being sued by employees, customers, or clients? Proactively demand arbitration agreements where contractual terms take the place of state law. What might have once been recognizable as corruption has become woven into legality. And in instances where an overburdened state can enforce some kind of oversight, billionaires and large corporations write off their fines and penalties as the cost of doing business. Neoliberalism's unraveling of sovereignty dismantles the social factory—much as leveraged buyouts enable financiers to buy up companies, saddle them with the debt that funded their purchase, sell off their assets, and fire their employees (perhaps hiring them back as benefitless temp workers and consultants).

The social factory—like the factory—was never merely despotic. Both point to productive relations between capital and labor, relations of exploitation within which labor, when unionized, has the leverage to exact concessions. Organized workers have some ability to shape the conditions of their exploitation, an ability "independent" contractors and workers in enterprise zones lack. This ability to extract concessions is true for the social factory as well. That democracy was the ideological form of exploitation placed conditions and expectations on that exploitation. Sovereignty wasn't just the sovereignty of the state. In its ideological form it was sovereignty of the people. With productive relations between capital and labor now subjected to expropriative relations of rent and service, the capacity to shape the conditions of life and work has dramatically diminished. Submission is the cost of doing business in a loose and unstable system of unequal and competing suzerainties.

The post-Fordist transformation in sovereignty is accompanied by a new prominence of violence. Negri associates this violence with the "re-emergence of the primitive accumulation model," the extraction rather than the production of value.[7] Finance itself functions extractively, enabling extreme concentrations of private assets. Here Negri's analysis aligns with Robert Brenner's account of the "politically driven upward redistribution of wealth."[8] Instead of rearranging production and implementing technological improvements to increase productivity, what Marx referred to as real subsumption, capital accumulation takes place under conditions of formal subsumption. Non-capitalist processes produce value that capital, whether via measures of finance or governance, simply takes. Examples of resurgent formal subsumption are Uber and Airbnb. Neither improve labor productivity or create new efficiencies in the provision of local transportation or lodging. Both rely on the fixed capital of earners rather than on capitalists who invest in means of production. Both turn assets acquired out of workers' consumption funds—their cars and houses—into means for the capital accumulation of another, the platform owner, as I detailed in chapter one.

Negri rightly draws out the extractive nature of capital accumulation under global financialization. But he also claims that "today exploitation no longer contains a contractual model."[9] It's more accurate to say that the function of the contract has shifted. It has shed the pretense of a contract between equals for an exchange of equivalents to become a means for intensified exploitation without the protective cover of public law. As Alain Supiot demonstrates, contractualization is a feature of a society of networks, deeply imbricated in the techniques "whereby people are *infeudalized* today."[10] Contemporary contracts lock people into "fulfilling objectives rather than observing rules."[11] Instead of functioning in terms of a law that obliges parties to do or refrain from doing something specific, contracts in networked society create a bond "which obliges one party to behave according to the expectations of the other."[12] When expectations aren't met, corrective mechanisms may be automatically triggered.

For Supiot, the shift from law to bond illustrates the way people come to be "placed in a network or relations of dependence." He explains:

> The guiding idea is not that all should be subject to the same abstract law, but that each person should behave in accordance with his or her place in the network. Each must do his best to serve the interests of those on whom he depends and be able to count on the loyalty of those who are dependent on him. People's legal status in their mutual relations and their relations to things is defined not by subordination to the same impersonal law, but by personal ties.[13]

Relational contracts bind people to the service of another in a contemporary version of vassalage. In its Western European form, vassalage was a legal contract though which one person is made dependent on another, as in homage or serfdom. This personal dimension of the bond was accompanied by a real or material dimension—the possession granted to the dependent. Such possession was always burdened with obligations, requirements of service to the other party. What the services entailed was determined by status. A serf might be required to perform agricultural labor while acts of loyalty service would be expected of a vassal.

Supiot sees an extension of vassalage in the contemporary shift from sovereignty to suzerainty. He writes, "The suzerain has immediate authority over his vassals, but not his vassals' vassals, whereas the sovereign's power is supreme—self-positing and bearing its cause within itself—and can be exercised directly over all his subjects."[14] Supiot's examples of contemporary suzerainty are the European Union and International Monetary Fund (IMF). Neither the EU nor its member states are sovereign; member states are in the position of vassals. With no direct authority over populations, the EU depends on the mediation of the member states. States swear allegiance to the IMF, subjecting themselves to carry out its requirements.

Despite the hopes and dreams of many an anarchist, the end of sovereignty is not a story of liberation. The unraveling of the state under conditions of capitalism's becoming neofeudal is a story of the loss of the universal amid fragmentation and privatization. Neoliberal policies aiming to shield capital, property, and markets from popular power open up new opportunities for private power to exert itself. Nesting fiefdoms and relations of vassalage sit within flows of conflict and alliance, armed empires and private militaries, algorithmically managed service and servitude. State power takes the form of suzerainty, and the social factory becomes a social manor. This is the background against which I now turn to the basic features of neofeudalism.

Parcellated sovereignty

Perry Anderson characterizes the feudal mode of production in Europe in terms of the parcellization of sovereignty.[15] Power was fragmented into multiple and shifting loci, configured in conditional, nested relationships of vassalage, service, and alliance. Ellen Meiksins Wood refines the idea of parcellated sovereignty by highlighting the "extra-economic coercion" that lords exerted over peasants.[16] Through traditional, legal, and political means, dispersed lords extracted surplus from the peasants on which they depended. Rather than a state collecting taxes or an employer paying wages, lords generally took the products of peasant labor in the form of rents, whether these were labor rents, money rents, or some combination thereof.

Lords' relations to peasants were both legal and economic, combining "the private exploitation of labor with the public role of administration, jurisdiction, and enforcement." [17] This public role was not determined by generally applicable public laws; it was up to the lords to administer, judge, and enforce as they chose. Because lordship involved a personal relation to peasants and property, contracts we may be accustomed to thinking of in terms of law in fact should be understood as taking the form of bonds. Disputes would be addressed by arbitration and compromise, determined by status and the specifics of a situation rather than by general legal norms. Not surprisingly, the line between legal and illegal was indistinct.

These two aspects of parcellated sovereignty—fragmentation and extra-economic coercion—appear in contemporary neofeudalization. As various scholars have observed, fragmentation occurs as private commercial interests displace public law. Chiara Cordelli argues that the impact of neoliberalism has been "a renewed feudal order within which political power is increasingly exercised on the basis of privately negotiated obligations, nonpublic purposes, and, ultimately, unilateral determinations." [18] Slobodian describes the myriad hybrid political and economic forms through which capital seeks to escape regulation: free ports, duty-free districts, city-states, gated communities, tax havens, innovation hubs, cryptocurrencies, and a dizzying array of zones (the most familiar being special economic zones and export-processing zones). [19] Robert Kuttner and Katherine Stone find that confidentiality agreements, non-compete rules, compulsory arbitration, the dismantling of public regulatory agencies, and the undermining of public education via vouchers and charter schools all exemplify ways that "legally sanctioned private jurisprudence—neo-feudalism" gives private entities power previously exercised by the state. [20]

With the parcellization of sovereignty, political authority and economic power blend together. The legal fictions of a bourgeois state determined by the forms of neutral law and free and equal individuals break down and the directly political character of society reasserts itself. Political power is exercised with and as economic power, not taxes but tolls, fines, liens, asset seizures, licenses, patents, jurisdictions, sanctions, and borders. The blurring of the political and the economic renders any political claim immediately self-interested and suspect, an instantiation of power, privilege, and bias.

The undermining of workers' rights due to the rise of compulsory arbitration is a particularly powerful example of the impact of neofeudalization on everyday life.[21] Over 55 percent of US workers are subject to mandatory arbitration agreements.[22] As a condition of employment, workers are made to sign an agreement that they will submit to arbitration in the event of a workplace dispute. For the sake of a job, they are compelled to give up their legal right to have their grievances adjudicated in a public court of law. This includes the right to engage in a class-action dispute—that is, a collective action regarding workplace and employment practices. Arbitration agreements are not confined to high-income, deeply specialized, or creative occupations. On the contrary, industries with large numbers of low-wage workers are the ones most frequently subjecting workers to mandatory arbitration agreements, in other words, industries whose workers are most dependent on their jobs for survival and least able to find other work. As in the feudal arrangement, so in the neofeudal do private economic actors exercise political power—the power to adjudicate disputes—over a particular group of people on the basis of terms and conditions that they, the private economic actors, set.

In the same vein, foreign investors have the right to sue state governments in international tribunals. The investor-state dispute settlement (ISDS) system allows foreign investors to sidestep domestic law and bring a claim against a country they've invested in if they think that country has violated the terms set out in specific bilateral investment treaties (BITs) or regional trade agreements (RTAs). The typical suit involves a corporation invoking ISDS when a state passes public-interest regulations designed to protect water, communities, or the environment. In suits against Latin American governments, Canadian mining exploration firms have brought a large number of such cases to arbitration tribunals. According to Manuel Perez-Rocha and Jen Moore, "The tribunal members are highly paid corporate lawyers who have no obligation to consider the rights of local communities or the importance of health and environmental protections."[23] The disputes are settled via arbitration agreements "that tend to be highly arbitrary, opaque, not open to public scrutiny, and generally pro-investor in their judgments."[24]

The implementation of the African Free Trade Agreement in 2021 occasioned the proliferation of arbitration courts across the continent. Not only are vastly unequal countries brought into a single market that benefits more established players such as South Africa, but the laws of the fifty-five countries in the agreement (the only country not part of it is Eritrea) can be limited or eclipsed in arbitration. These elements of the architecture of global trade, Jayati Ghosh writes, "are about protecting and promoting private investment, of all types, and effectively privileging the rights of investors over the rights of citizens in the host country."[25] Private economic power trumps public law, not only decreasing the policy options available to states but actively dismantling even the fiction of popular sovereignty.

The explosion in financial technology—"fintech"—is a creepy reflexivization of neofeudalism's patterns of blending economic and privatized social coercion: our data (which we give up unaware or under arcane user agreements over which we have no control) gets linked to our credit worthiness. Apps for securing easy credit mine users' smartphone data and track their interactions for indications of how desperate they might be for a loan and how risky that loan might be. In Kenya, fintech's predatory micro-lending created an epidemic of indebtedness. Companies like Safara.com (one of the largest corporations in East Africa), Tala, and Branch (headquartered in California) offer financially strapped Kenyans small loans to help get them through the month, locking them into perpetual indebtedness with exorbitant interest rates and further impacting their credit rating. How do these private companies get away with this? According to Kevin P. Donovan and Emma Park, it's because of their "capacity to escape jurisdiction," a capacity that is both cause and effect of parcellated sovereignty.[26]

Ten percent of global wealth is hoarded in offshore accounts to avoid taxation—that is, to escape the reach of state law. Law doesn't apply to billionaires powerful enough to evade it. Libertarians try to gin up enthusiasm for cryptocurrencies on the basis of the capacity of blockchain and similar consensus algorithms to circumvent state power. Correlatively, the largest tech companies have valuations greater than the economies of most of the world's countries. Cities and states relate to Apple, Amazon, Microsoft, Facebook (Meta), and Google (Alphabet) as if these corporations were themselves sovereign states, trying to attract and negotiate with these firms on the firms' own terms. Governments auction off control over their political economy in the form of subsidies and tax breaks, which puts them in a position where they can no longer meet basic social needs and so remain bound to private firms until the firms decide to leave. Firms exploit this dependence, using the threat of departure to extort more concessions from dependent governments (which should really no longer be seen as governments; they are managers overseeing the "non-government of domination" that Rahmane Idrissa associates with feudal colonialism in the Sahel). Immense concentrated wealth has its own constituent power, the power to constitute the rules it will follow—or not.

Kuttner and Stone use Mortgage Electronic Registration Services (MERS) to illustrate how the blending of economic and political power characteristic of neofeudalism's parcellated sovereignty effaces the distinction between legal and illegal. A shell company, MERS was a private database created and owned by big banks. Its purpose was avoiding the fees associated with traditional practices of registering mortgages. During the housing bubble leading up to the crisis of 2008, banks encouraged the buying and selling of mortgages so that they could combine these mortgages into securitized assets. MERS let them list just the original mortgage; when banks sold mortgages to other banks—which they did multiple times—they could list MERS as the lender. When the financial crisis hit, MERS was the source of countless problems, from database errors to unlawful mortgage transfers. Millions of people found themselves in foreclosure proceedings and lost their homes "based on fraudulent documents from a shell company that was at best a legal fiction."[27] A private system for designating property took over what had been a public legal domain. The result was the illegal expropriation of people's homes.

The widespread privatization of state functions testifies to sovereignty's fragmentation. Privatization has been a widely discussed dimension of neoliberalism, from the dismantling of state socialism in the former Eastern Bloc to the forcing of structural adjustment policies onto the Global South and the imposition of austerity in the EU and elsewhere. Security is one of the most visible domains of privatization. Already in the early 2000s, scholars in international relations and security studies were documenting the unraveling of the state's monopoly on the legitimate use of violence within a given territory.[28] Marina Caparini identifies a pluralization of security within states and transnationally, as authority is fragmented across public and private actors at local, state, and international levels.[29] From above, states outsource military and security tasks to private commercial firms. From below, insurgents, militias, gangs, and other opposition groups both challenge the state and fill in for its retreat and incapacity.

That the blurring of political authority and economic power erodes legality is widely apparent. Palestine is the most obvious example, as Israeli settlers illegally build up settlements on Palestinian land, protected by Israeli military forces. There are patterns here, as the activist slogan "From Ferguson to Palestine, occupation is a crime!" announces. The dramatic expansion of misdemeanor law in the already enormous US carceral system illustrates the point. Poor people, disproportionately people of color, are arrested on bogus charges and convinced to plead guilty so as to avoid the jail time they could incur should they contest the charges. Not only does the guilty plea go on their record, but they start to accrue fines that, if they can't afford to pay them, will result in more fines and more charges. The legal system itself operates as a mode of expropriation. We got a brief look at this system in the wake of the 2014 riots in Ferguson, Missouri, that followed the murder of Michael Brown: "The city's municipal court and policing apparatus openly extracted millions of dollars from its low-income African American population."[30] Police were instructed "to make arrests and issue citations in order to raise revenue." Like vassals of feudal lords, police forcibly expropriate surplus from the people.

As the shift from sovereignty to suzerainty suggests, feudal social relations are distinguished by the absence of centralized public power and the intermeshing of economic and political power. In the twenty-first century, similar phenomena of fragmentation and political and economic blending pervade the globe. Imperialist states like the US place economic sanctions on weaker states, starving, brutalizing, and killing civilian populations in a neofeudal version of medieval siege warfare.[31] As Jessica Whyte details in a study of the devastating impact of US unilateral coercive measures on Venezuela, international law has been ill equipped at dealing with a form of power that blurs the line between permitted economic competition and prohibited political coercion. She writes:

> By preventing countries from restructuring their debts, financial sanctions push them into default, generating spiraling interest rates and capital flight. By freezing central bank funds, they deprive countries of the resources to defend their currencies. And by weaponizing inflation and unemployment, they ensure that, even when food and medicine is available, it is too expensive for most civilians to afford.[32]

The fiction of a political system anchored in the rule of law and an economic system following capitalist laws of motion gives way to networked private relations in which power and privilege reign.

New lords and serfs

The second feature of neofeudalism concerns social property relations. I use "new lords and serfs" to designate neofeudalism's forms of hierarchy and expropriation. Our present is structured around the concentration of wealth in the hands of billionaires and the concentration of labor in services. Recent decades have witnessed increasing distance between rich and poor, owners and renters, a separation aided by a differentiated legal architecture that protects corporations and wealthy asset holders while it immiserates and incarcerates the working and lower class. In the US, the entrenchment of economic inequality is severe: the US has less economic mobility than England, a country with a landed aristocracy.

David Graeber was attentive to the feudal character of the rise of services. Recognizing how contemporary corporations are less involved in making and more involved in "political processes of appropriating, distributing, and allocating money and resources," Graeber identified managerialism as a new form of feudalism.[33] Crucial to this form is the proliferation of bullshit jobs, endless degrees of hierarchy where power and prestige are determined by the numbers of underlings and reportages. Capitalist economies driven by goals of efficiency and profit maximization should be immunized from the accumulation of unproductive vassals and retainers. One explanation for the accumulation of such positions is that the system isn't capitalist.[34]

Services are a broad and heterogeneous category, spanning from the highly paid legal and financial retainers who enable asset holders to retain their class privilege to the enormous expanse of informal and low-waged cleaners, childminders, cooks, and drivers. Over the next ten years, the occupation that will add the most jobs in the US is personal care aides, not health workers but aides who bathe and clean people. Another age would call them servants.[35] Many people newly pushed into service work find that their phones, bikes, cars, and homes have lost their character as personal property and been transformed into instruments of labor and means for the continued extraction of additional rents and fees. Tethered to platforms owned by others, consumer items and means of life are means for the platform owners' accumulation.

Not only do most of us constitute a propertyless underclass able to survive only by servicing the needs of high earners, but we often find ourselves caught in labor relations where we pay for the opportunity to work. Self-employed personal trainers (SEPTs) illustrate the point. In their study of precarious work in fitness centers, Geraint Harvey and his coauthors outline a form of "neo-villeiny" characterized by a bond to an organization and its physical resources, payment of rents, income insecurity, and extensive unpaid work.[36] SEPTs generally work out of fitness centers to which they pay rents and on which they depend for access to clients and equipment. They take on various unpaid tasks (cleaning up, answering phones, maintaining an upbeat atmosphere) for the benefit of the organization and assume the financial risks associated with the lack of a guaranteed income. More broadly, some of us enjoy the fantasy that our service is creative, that we are members of a privileged class of knowledge workers. Yet as with SEPTs, much of that work is done for free, for the chance of pay, rarely with a chance of security. Knowledge workers, like day laborers, compete for contracts—if we win, we get to work more.

An international unevenness is constitutive of neofeudalism. Viewing tourism as a vehicle for economic growth, governments prioritize servicing the desires of travelers rather than meeting the needs of their own people, remaking populations of workers (whether craft, agricultural, or industrial) into servants of the privileged. The Philippines relies on income that domestic workers earn abroad. Nearly 9 percent of the country's GDP comes from Filipina women serving a privileged global elite.[37] Interactions between governments and corporations also illustrate the international unevenness constitutive of neofeudalism. A report on extractive industries prepared for the African Commission on Human and People's Rights, for instance, highlights the clientelist relations between multinational corporations and African governments. It argues that the dependence of these states on the income generated from extractive resources risks turning them into "rental fiefdoms—where the political elite buy support instead of investing in sound economic policies."[38] A final illustration of the international unevenness constitutive of neofeudalism is de-development in the Arab world. Ali Kadri details how Arab states, beholden to US capital and security, are dependently tied to an imperialist world economy in which accumulation comes from "violent social dislocation, value grab structured around oil, and commercial as opposed to industrial activity."[39] Accumulation isn't capitalistic. It's driven by a "belligerent encroachment and dislocation" that subsumes "Third World labor and resources to US-led capital."[40]

The international class of super-rich asset holders are increasingly shielded from the rest of us. Their planes are private, schools are private, clubs are private. Even their spaceships are private. They rely on private security, personal bodyguards. Operating as a global ruling class, they make their fortunes through the proliferation of mechanisms of direct expropriation: bank fees for every possible transaction, illegal foreclosures and evictions, the disaggregation of services into separate chargeable elements, direct wage theft—which is frequent, widespread, and impossible for people who can't afford lawyers to combat. Under neoliberalism, wealth holders have been particularly successful at using the state to increase their share of the social surplus. The US government redistributes taxes on people to corporations. In 2018, for example, fifty-seven corporations, including Amazon, not only didn't pay taxes but received tax rebates. Society is structured to systematically take from the poor and give to the rich—the higher cost of food and transportation in underserved areas, excessive interest on loans, rent paid weekly when one doesn't have strong enough credit to secure a longer-term lease, and so on. This same structure repeats on an international scale with entire countries forced to gut their social provisioning as they capitulate to powerful creditors.

As in earlier European feudalism, land plays a role in neofeudalism, but the role is different—now it's a way to hoard assets more than it is a means for driving agricultural production. Over the past forty years more than 2 million hectares of British public land (10 percent of Britain's overall land mass) have been sold to private buyers. According to

Brett Christophers, this sell-off has occurred at various levels, from local to national, for various reasons, and under various auspices in a "piecemeal and fragmented process" (parcellated sovereignty).[41] In the US, land is also increasingly privatized: 100 families own about 42 million acres, the equivalent of 65,000 square miles. Christophers rightly points out that Marx saw the enclosure of the commons as a crucial condition for capitalist development insofar as this enclosure threw peasants off the land and forced them to sell their labor power in order to survive. The new round of privatization is different. The rise in private-sector land-hoarding has transformed Britain into a rentier economy where the many pay rent to the already affluent landowning few. Since the land isn't put to productive use, enclosure isn't benefiting capital; it's following and intensifying neofeudal laws of motion.

While there has been widespread land-hoarding on the part of the super-rich, the primary mode of surplus extraction today is not a landed aristocracy sitting on a peasant class legally bound to the land (even as the largest landowner in the world is the King of England; the British royal family owns more than 6.6 billion acres of land). Neofeudalism does not designate the simple return of the feudal form of expropriation. In the so-called advanced economies, the majority of people do not have direct access to their means of reproduction. They require some kind of income that will enable them to purchase what they need to subsist—food, shelter, and means of life. Neofeudal serfs are proletarianized serfs, "free" from the land, "free" from job security, "free" from social-welfare safety nets, and dependent on markets for every aspect of their lives. Although this "freedom" makes them look like the proletarians Marx described, they are integrated into laws of motion that have little to do with capital's compulsions to maximize profit and increase labor productivity by investing in means of production. Not only do today's proletarianized neoserfs labor in the low-productivity services that have come to predominate in deindustrialized societies, but many labor in settings where they are not employed by capitalists at all: they pay for the opportunity to sell their labor to consumers of services. If under capitalism we sell ourselves, under neofeudalism we pay a fee to access a market where we can sell ourselves.

Networked telecommunications have enabled the insertion of a new class of appropriators who accumulate by charging for access to markets. This is what platforms like Google, Facebook, Amazon, Apple's App Store, Uber, and Airbnb provide—"digital infrastructures that enable two or more groups to interact" (to use Nick Srnicek's definition of a platform).[42] Platforms position themselves between buyers and sellers, seekers and suppliers, mediating interactions while collecting fees and data. Platforms' monopoly power and enormous infrastructures produce ecosystems that shape economic life in ways impossible to escape. Even though technology companies employ a relatively small percentage of the workforce, their effects are tremendous, essentially remaking entire industries around the acquisition, mining, and deployment of data. It's because of the smaller workforces that data tech is indicative of a tendency to neofeudalism. Accumulation occurs less through commodity production and wage labor than through rents, licenses, fees, work done for free, and data treated as a natural resource. Those who work for a wage are subjected to ever-worsening conditions as algorithmic scheduling and surveillance technology press them to work harder and faster, with few breaks and fewer benefits. For workers in Amazon warehouses, call centers, and fast food, work is degrading, soul sucking, abusive, and literally dehumanizing: that people tire, use the toilet, can't always work to full capacity, and have lives isn't part of the equation.[43]

Crucial to the power of platforms is the way they constitute grounds for user activities; platforms are the conditions of possibility for interactions to occur. Google makes it possible to find information in an impossibly dense and changing information environment. Amazon lets us easily locate consumer goods, compare prices, and purchase these goods from established as well as unknown vendors. Uber enables strangers to share rides. Airbnb does the same for houses and apartments. One's car isn't for personal transport. It's for making money. One's apartment isn't a place to live; it's something to rent out. Personal property becomes an instrument for the capital and data accumulation of the lords of platform. The more people use these platforms, the less we can avoid them. The platforms become more effective, more powerful, ultimately transforming the larger environment of which they are a part. Airbnb comes into an area, forcing up rents and property valuations. Now to afford rents or taxes, one has to Airbnb.

Consider Amazon. Stacy Mitchell describes it as a toll road.[44] It extracts enormous fees from the merchants wanting to sell goods in its marketplace. These include the fee to sell on the site, called a referral fee, and two "optional fees"—advertising and fulfillment. Because of Amazon's practice of prioritizing sponsored ads in search results, sellers feel compelled to buy additional advertising (instead of relying on customer ratings to elevate their position). Many sellers have also turned to Amazon for warehousing and shipping, Fulfillment by Amazon (FBA). Again, this is because the algorithms prioritize FBA sellers in search results. Selling on other sites is barely an option: not only does Amazon's domination of the online sales market render other sales outlets less viable and harder to find, but sellers can't lower their prices on these other outlets. Amazon's "competitive pricing" rules demote the items in search results, eliminate the "buy now" button, and add an alert that tells customers that the item is priced higher on Amazon than on other sites (disincentivizing sellers from using sites where they can charge less). Amazon is literally controlling access to the market.

Amazon's aggressive fee structure enables additional predatory practices. Amazon loses billions with the free shipping promised by its Prime subscription service. The popular service, though, is what lets Amazon maintain its dominance in online sales. Customers have strong incentives to shop on Amazon when they've paid for Prime. The enormous sums that seller fees generate more than make up for the Prime losses. In fact, the fees for advertising, warehousing, and shipping actually paid for Amazon's enormous logistics buildup. In effect, Amazon pushed the costs onto its sellers. They built the infrastructure they had no choice but to use.

Amazon's fees and tolls combine with the rent-driven accumulation strategy of Amazon Web Services (AWS). Like Azure (Microsoft) and GCP (Google), AWS is a cloud platform. Users are charged for processing (called "compute"), networking (input and output), and storage. Instead of building up their own technological infrastructures, firms purchase computing services from larger tech companies. The big three tech companies control about 65 percent of the cloud market. If a smaller competitor poses a risk, one of them buys it. Functioning like public utilities in that they provide essential services too expensive for most firms to supply for themselves, the structural dominance of these companies—and the fact that they *aren't* public utilities—enables them to act in predatory and unaccountable ways.

With the development of machine learning and generative artificial intelligence (AI), the power asymmetries seem insurmountably immense. Developing and training deep-learning applications requires enormous data sets and amounts of compute. Only a few companies are in a position to provide, much less afford, it. OpenAI—which developed and released the groundbreaking ChatGPT—uses Azure; Microsoft invested $10 billion in the company, acquiring a 49 percent share.[45]

Lordship designates a social relation for the appropriation of surplus. Are we not in that same relation with big tech? The theme of peasants and lords of the internet that Jaron Lanier noted in 2010 has escalated to become widely accepted common sense as the tech giants have grown richer and more extractive because their structural dominance enables them to exact increasingly unavoidable tolls, fees, and rents. Neither consumers nor businesses can avoid them, and cities and states compete to attract them. The economic scale and impact of our tech overlords is greater than that of most so-called sovereign states. Like so many tributary demands, their tax breaks take money from communities. Their presence drives up rents and real estate prices, driving out affordable apartments, small businesses, and people. Shoshana Zuboff's study of "surveillance capitalism" brings out a further neofeudal element of tech lordship—military service.[46] Like powerful lords to needy kings, Facebook and Google cooperate with state governments, tracking perceived enemies, reporting their activities, and crippling their ability to communicate by removing their sites or blocking their access.

Hinterlandization

The third attribute of neofeudalism concerns its spatiality. Ellen Meiksins Wood tells us that medieval European cities were essentially oligarchies, "with dominant classes enriched by commerce and financial services for kings, emperors, and popes. Collectively, they dominated the surrounding countryside . . . extracting wealth from it in one way or another."[47] Today we again encounter a political and economic landscape where desolate hinterlands surround protected, often lively, centers. Alec MacGillis describes "winner-take-all cities" like San Francisco, Boston, New York, and Washington, DC, surrounded by "underpopulated towns blasted by the opioid scourge and bereft of any retail except the omnipresent chain dollar store."[48] He makes clear that the urban-rural divide today is also an urban-urban divide between the cities that are left behind and the cities in which capital concentrates. This division repeats within winner cities as gentrification makes some areas unaffordable and other ones barely habitable. Public space declines and private spaces become mini fortresses oriented toward protecting the rich and their assets, services available to the rich depending on what they are willing to pay. Rowland Atkinson points to the displays of prestige emblazoned throughout the hyper-secure residential landscape, viewing them as indicative of a "lord of the manor syndrome."[49] A city gets richer, more people become displaced, dispossessed, and houseless, and elites engage in new forms of castellation.

The US hinterlands are sites of loss and dismantlement, places with fantasies of a flourishing capitalist past that for a while might have let some linger in the hope that their lives and their children's lives might actually get better. Emily Guendelsberger writes in *On the Clock*, "I've seen so many ghost towns and shuttered factories in Kentucky, Indiana, and North Carolina—just drive twenty minutes in any direction, they're everywhere."[50] Remnants of an industrial capitalism that's left them behind in search of a more reliable mode of accumulation, the hinterlands are ripe for the new intensified exploitation that looks like something worse than capitalism. No longer making things, people persist through warehouses, call centers, dollar stores, and fast food. "Most fulfillment centers are pretty remote," Guendelsberger tells us in her account of working at Amazon for one of the temp agencies that provide warehouse workers during the holiday rush.[51]

Politically, the desperation of the hinterlands manifests in the political movements of those outside the cities, movements that are sometimes around environmental issues (fracking and pipeline struggles), sometimes around land (privatization and expropriation), and sometimes around the reduction of services (hospital and school closings). In the US, the politics of guns positions the hinterlands against the urban: rural and suburban gun owners view even the most minimal regulatory efforts as threats to their individual capacity to defend themselves in a violent and lawless society.

We should read the increased prominence of social reproduction theory as a response to hinterlandization—that is, as a response to the loss of a general capacity to reproduce the basic conditions of livable life. This appears in rising suicide rates, increasing anxiety and drug addiction, declining birth rates, lowering rates of life expectancy, and, in the US, the psychotic societal self-destruction of mass shootings. It appears in the collapsed infrastructures and undrinkable water. The hinterlands are written on people's bodies and on the land. With closures of hospitals and schools, and the diminution of basic services, life becomes more desperate and uncertain. Strikes of teachers and nurses in the US have made their primary demands not simply better salaries, staffing, and working conditions—although these matter—but improved conditions for students and patients. The crisis of care links providers and recipients of care work, exposing the structural conditions of neofeudalizing capitalism.

Phil A. Neel's *Hinterland* observes patterns between China, Egypt, Ukraine, and the United States. They are all places with desolate abandoned wastelands and cities on the brink of overload. Neel's account of stratification and struggle across the international periphery echoes arguments made by international relations scholars thirty years earlier. Already in 1998, Philip Cerny was writing of the "growing alienation between global innovation, communication and resource nodes (global cities) on the one hand and disfavored, fragmented hinterlands on the other."[52] Cerny warned of the resulting exclusion and lumpenization. As large geographical spaces are starved of infrastructure and support, he said, "many people will simply be 'out of the loop,' country bumpkins or even roaming deprived bands . . . forced once again to become predators or supplicants on the cities, as in the Middle Ages."[53]

Correlative to the divisions between what is secured and what is endangered, who is prosperous and who is desperate, are the nomads and migrants seeking life and work and coming up against borders and walls. Their real conditions at the edge of survival become mirrored back to them in the fears of the protected, who can never be safe enough—which leads me to the fourth characteristic of neofeudalism: catastrophic anxiety.

Catastrophic anxiety

The fourth characteristic takes us to affective dimensions of neofeudalism, the pervasive feelings of insecurity, anxiety, and catastrophe. Umair Haque describes the "existential traumatic shock" behind the regressive anti-revolutions associated with Bolsonaro, Trump, Modi, Brexit, QAnon, anti-maskers, and anti-vaxxers. Haque uses the example of the average American lacking the savings or social safety net necessary for weathering everyday crises like a medical emergency, home or car repair, death in the family, or job loss: "Life is marked by constant dread and anxiety and panic, not over anything that might come to be—but things that *must* be, things for which there is no escape, like death, birth, and illness. Simply existing itself is a task, an ever-growing burden, both economic and psychic."[54] Haque sees the average American as a powerless "neo-serf"—"a creation unique in modern history—a nominal citizen of a rich country, but one whose every imaginable possibility goes on shrinking by the day . . . because he is impotent, castrated, every day can only feel something like either torment or death." People have good reasons for feeling insecure. The catastrophe of neofeudal capitalism's expropriation of the social surplus in the setting of a grossly unequal and warming planet is real.

An embrace of the cryptic, occult, techno-pagan, and anti-modern amplifies apocalyptic insecurity. Adherents to the QAnon conspiracy theory read breadcrumbs dropped on online message boards for clues that will help them understand power relations. Prophets and evangelists operating outside of institutional religion offer healing, visions, and predictions. In the US, interest in prophecy has expanded into movement proportions.[55] Globally, fear of and interest in witches is rising. According to Bianca Bosker, "The latest witch renaissance coincides with a growing fascination with astrology, crystals, and tarot, which, like magic, practitioners consider ways to tap into unseen, unconventional sources of power—and which can be especially appealing for people who feel disenfranchised or who have grown weary of trying to enact change by working within the system."[56] Pervasive mistrust of government science exacerbated the COVID-19 pandemic. People with little confidence in experts—their lack of confidence reinforced by then president Donald Trump—embraced pseudoscientific coronavirus denialism as well as fake remedies. We can add to this mix Jordan Peterson's mystical Jungianism, Nick Land's "dark enlightenment," and Aleksandr Dugin's mythical geopolitics of Atlantis and Hyperborea.

Peter Thiel, the billionaire founder of PayPal and Palantir Technologies, pushes an explicitly neofeudal worldview. In a lecture in 2012, Thiel explained the link between feudalism and tech start-ups: "No founder or CEO has absolute power. It's more like the archaic feudal structure. People vest the top person with all sorts of power and ability, and then blame them if and when things go wrong."[57] What's interesting here is how feudal structure is rendered as an instrument of freedom, a move Corey Robin associates with American "democratic feudalism" where the "promise of democracy is to govern another human being as completely as a monarch governs his subjects."[58] While Thiel is happy to jettison the democratic element altogether, he shares the view that freedom is the protection of privilege and that privileges are the expression of an inner genius. Along with other Silicon Valley capitalists, Thiel wants to protect his fortune from democratic impingement and so advocates strategies of exodus and isolation such as living on the sea and space colonization, whatever it takes to save wealth from taxation. Extreme capitalism goes over into the radical decentralization of neofeudalism as tech lords fortify their holdings outside the reach of the state.

For those on the other side of the neofeudal divide, anxiety and insecurity are addressed less by ideology than by opioids, alcohol, and food, anything to dull the pain of hopeless, mindless, endless drudgery. Guendelsberger describes the stress caused by constant technological surveillance on the job—the risk of being fired for being a few seconds late, for not meeting quotas, for using the bathroom too many times. Repetitive, low-control, high-stress work like the kind that is technologically monitored correlates directly with depression and anxiety. Uncertain schedules (lauded as flexible) and unreliable pay (because wage theft is ubiquitous and work isn't guaranteed) are stressful, deadening. Neofeudal apocalypticism can be individual, familial, local. It's hard to get worked up about a climate catastrophe when you've lived catastrophe for a few generations.

Haque's emphasis on the regressive politics of contemporary anti-revolutions makes the link between catastrophism and feudalism. Trumpism, he writes, "hopes to make today's impoverished, powerless neo-serf tomorrow's little tribal master over immigrants and minorities. Feudalism is the goal of these anti-revolutions, in which the neo-serf becomes a chieftain in his own right, one of the pure in a promised land."[59] Resonating with Robin's theorization of American democratic feudalism, Haque's analysis lets us see the appeal of neofeudalism to those who find themselves dominated and constrained. If one isn't free to control another person, one isn't free.

The COVID-19 pandemic amplified the sense of epochal crisis, not only as it realized the global spread of a deadly, contagious, airborne virus, already a Hollywood trope, but as millions became infected and died, bodies piling up, countries shutting down, the fault lines of the underlying system as vulnerable and exposed as any emergency room nurse. Darko Suvin highlights the role of neofeudal land-hoarding in the pandemic: global agribusiness's land grabs and deforestation release pathogens from their former isolation into the human food chain.[60] The pandemic wasn't caused by the virus alone. It resulted from market-driven agriculture, economic immiseration, megacities, slums, degenerated health care, and the global movement of people and products. Such conditions produce pandemics out of viruses.[61] What Suvin calls "coronization" revealed neoliberal austerity as a policy of mass murder: privatized, diminished, and underfunded healthcare systems failed to meet basic needs. In societies of abundance, there weren't enough beds, ventilators, oxygen, masks, or medical staff. The pandemic demonstrated that essential workers are the most exploited workers, the ones forced to work and left to die. Coronization revealed the political domination of death cults in the US, the UK, and Brazil. Risking death was treated as a liberating experience of freedom, especially for those able to purchase the means of survival. The culling of everyone else was just what was necessary to achieve herd immunity.

During the mass uprising that followed the police murder of George Floyd in May 2020, Black Lives Matter demonstrations in my small city took the form of nightly processions throughout the neighborhoods. Accompanied by the steady drumbeat of pots and pans, people chanted, "I can't breathe"; "Black Lives Matter"; and "We are here." The masks and persistent clanging, the congregating in the wake of fear of infection, gave the processions a medieval vibe. They sometimes felt more like supplications challenging the death cults than political demonstrations. Maybe it's better to say that challenging the order of death is a form politics takes in neofeudal times. This might be one explanation for the intensity of the global movement to stop Israel's genocide against the Palestinians that grew throughout the fall of 2023 and into 2024.

Neofeudalism's catastrophic anxiety flourishes in the affective infrastructures of communicative capitalism where there is no commonly shared meaning. Lies circulate as easily as or more easily than truth—especially when there is nothing to stabilize or guarantee truth, no generally accepted procedures of verification. Outrage trumps reason and nuance. With constant communication but maddening incommunicability, we lose the sense not just that no one hears us but that even if they do, there is no way they can understand us. Meaning is individuated; what matters to me, what I have experienced, what I feel. Under these conditions of what Slavoj Žižek calls the "decline of symbolic efficiency," disparate issues and concerns are equalized—the daily deaths of thousands circulating in the same media space as fury over word choice and straight-up lies. Little registers as significant—or everything is equally significant—because signification has become so elusive.

This fragmentation of the symbolic is another dimension of the parcellation of sovereignty—the parcellation of the big Other. No master signifier holds meaning together, just as there is no sovereign law but instead extensive forms of legal privatization and personalized networks of fealty and privilege. Under these fragmented conditions, assuming that one will have one's day in court is naïve, a remnant of religious belief in Judgment Day. For most of us, being able to afford a lawyer when we need one—or having a lawyer that could secure us a fair trial rather than pressure us to take a plea deal—is a fantasy. We're resigned to the fact that the violations we experience—wage theft, denied insurance claims, unwanted sexual attention, unexpected and exorbitant medical bills—elude legal remedy.

The parcellation of the big Other manifests in countless ways. Rather than norms, there are exceptions. Zero-hour contracts are a well-known example: workers must be available for work they may not get. Other examples include higher education: final exams and final grades have lost their finality. Students request various accommodations and exemptions; they ask for extra credit, opportunities to resubmit work, reconsideration. Responding to the personal circumstances of each now appears fairer than subjecting all to a common set of requirements. Airline tickets are another example. Prices are disaggregated and personalized; there is not a standard charge that everyone pays. Airline ticket prices shift by the day, even hour, sometimes depending on prior searches. Once a quoted price is accepted, the purchaser will immediately be presented with multiple additional purchase options and fees. The purchased ticket can also change at any point as airlines cancel flights, change flight times, or rebook the flight through different airports. Practices that previously had the structure of a contract, whether implied or explicit, have a new degree of fluidity. Expectations of consistency— that someone will do what they've agreed, show up on time—now seem harsh, conservative, indifferent to the many personal things the other is dealing with. Or worse: keeping one's word is for suckers, those too weak to adjust the pact to their benefit.

No wonder so many of us lose the capacity to accept ambiguity, grabbing instead for an impossible certainty, even when, especially when, it is not widely shared but understood only by a few—prophets, witches, Q, and the crypto guys going on about blockchain. Noteworthy in all these instances is an intense attachment to a certain truth, an intensity that draws its energy from rejection of the common, mainstream, widely accepted, liberal, and democratic. We can add to this mix the shift from social construction to ontology as prominent reflexes in academic theorizing; appealing to an essence beyond politics and representation shores up our need for certainty in uncertain times. Correlative moves in the culture wars fixate on identity as a fundamental ground or guarantor, as if experience were clear and self-knowledge readily available.

In his seminar on anxiety, Lacan discusses the sense of certainty associated with "essentialist proofs" based in ideas of perfection of the sort offered by St. Anselm and Descartes. Lacan argues that the maintenance of this contestable certainty in the face of derision and scorn suggests that it's "a displacement, a certainty that is secondary in relation to the certainty of anxiety."[62] Doubt is an effort to combat this certainty of anxiety.[63] In contrast to our everyday conception of anxiety as a kind of paralyzing doubt, in Lacan's teaching doubt shields us from the more disquieting and uncanny certainty of anxiety.

Why is anxiety certain? Because it never deceives. Lacan's point involves language, signification, and the speaking subject. Subjects who speak are subjects who can lie. There is an irreducible gap between the speaker and the spoken. We can always ask: *Why are you telling me this*, or *What are you trying to achieve by telling me this?* Anxiety is the affect that accompanies signification, testifying to the signifier's "furrow in the real."[64] What the speaker says may be a lie; the words I hear might deceive me; my eyes might trick me. Anxiety, though, is a signal of the Real. More specifically, for Lacan it's the signal of the Real of enjoyment. As Lacan explains, Freud viewed anxiety as a reaction to the loss of an object—loss of the mother, of the penis, of love from the object. Lacan disagrees: "Anxiety isn't about the loss of the object, but its presence. The objects aren't missing."[65] Rather than lack, there is abundance, too much, an overwhelming degree of connection, envelopment, and potential absorption in the Other. Anxiety signals the lack of a lack, the risk of being captured in the Other's demand, of suffocating in their enjoyment. Anxiety is an affect that signals an encounter with the Real of jouissance.

It may be that the deep appeal of existential certainty today is the shadow of the certainty of anxiety. As the central affect in contemporary society, anxiety signals our inability to secure some kind of space where we are free of the Other's demand, shielded from their enjoyment. The shift from law to bond, from public to private jurisprudence, indexes the legal form of this insecurity. We have to abide by expectations, not clear and definable rules, and that means perpetually trying to decipher what the Other wants from us. Social networks tie us to so many others that the task is impossible, unfulfillable. Anxiety doesn't deceive. Put into the Other's service, we become nothing but instruments of their enjoyment, our servitude the condition of possibility for them to enjoy.

I've characterized neofeudalism as a shift from sovereignty to suzerainty. Neofeudalism has four basic features: parcellated sovereignty, new lords and serfs, hinterlandization, and catastrophic anxiety. My claim is not a historical one about feudalism's fundamental structure; it's that neofeudalism changes how we see capitalism by drawing out what it is becoming. Viewed as a neofeudalizing tendency, parcellization—fragmentation—is not to be embraced as democratic pluralization; it's the new structuring of economic and political power that drives advancing servitude and hinterlandization. Likewise, the rejection of reason and embrace of mysticism aren't indicative of creative flourishing; they correspond to the pervasive anxiety that accompanies the unceasing demands and unavoidable enjoyment that the decline of symbolic efficiency makes it impossible to escape. In the following chapter, I develop the repercussions of the decline of symbolic efficiency in neofeudalism's psychotic atmosphere—the absence of a neofeudal subject and the proliferation of fragile, rivalrous others.

4

The Subject Supposed to Care

"Nobody cares" is a common refrain, repeated in headlines, articles, and social media, about a wide array of issues that many people seem actually to care quite a lot about.[1] Nobody cares about the carers, about Haiti, about new COVID variants, about climate change. Nobody cares about political corruption, unraveling social institutions, scholasticide, gun violence, declining life expectancy, increasing suicide rates, rising anti-Semitism, fires in Canada, floods in Greece, recording-breaking temperatures in Pakistan. An article on why the Middle East doesn't fully support Ukraine quoted a young Syrian man at a café in Berlin: "Assad is still in power, the Russians still support him—and nobody cares."[2] A billionaire partial owner of the Golden State Warriors basketball team said, "Nobody cares about what's happening to the Uyghurs, okay. You bring it up because you really care, and I think it's nice that you really care, the rest of us don't care . . . I'm just telling you a hard, ugly truth. Of all the things I care about, yes, it's below my line."[3] On October 3, 2023, an opinion piece arguing that the best the Palestinians can hope for is "a reservation-type arrangement that the US gave Indians and the British gave the Aborigines" ran in the *Jewish Press*. The title: "The Palestinians: A People about Whom Nobody Cares."[4] Seven months later, the *New York Times* quoted Ra'fat Abu Tueima, one of 600,000 Palestinians pushed out of Rafah— which had previously been declared a safe zone—by Israeli tanks and air strikes. Because of Israel's US-backed onslaught on Gaza, he and his family of nine children had been forced to move six times. Abu Tueima said: "No one even cares about all those women and children here."[5] Since the issues and events about which no one allegedly cares are actually matters about which some people care quite deeply, why is the sentiment that "nobody cares" ubiquitous?

My argument is that "nobody cares" points to the decline of symbolic efficiency, the absence of a symbolic space of registration that functions as the background knowledge that one can assume that others accept. There's no big Other who cares or who sees us caring. Little others may care, but that's not enough to assuage the feeling that, when it comes right down to it, we are on our own, especially with respect to the fundamental conditions of our lives. Everything feels chaotic. We're awash in vibes without agency, submerged in catastrophic forces beyond our control. The subject of neofeudalism is missing because there's no big Other who can see it.

Neofeudalism's affective infrastructure

The neofeudal social manor is populated by fragile, competitive others struggling within a broader landscape of anxiety, fragmentation, shamelessness, and hierarchic dependence. Its affective infrastructure is built on what Lacanian psychoanalysis describes as the imaginary plane, a register of identification, aggression, and rivalry. Exploring this infrastructure involves tracking the effects of declining symbolic efficiency in a setting where capitalism is increasingly no longer recognizably capitalist, but something worse. Rather than reliant on a subject in the sense of modernity's disciplined citizen or psychoanalysis's neurotic (which are the same), neofeudalism absorbs us in a psychotic atmosphere of unrelenting demands and overwhelming enjoyment in a setting lacking symbolic bearings.

Lacan distinguishes between the normal and the psychotic subject. The normal subject goes about their business in an uncertain world, not questioning everything too closely, accepting a kind of "good enough" consensus about the way the world works. Unable to access the commonly accepted symbolic order, the psychotic creates a delusion, becoming fixated on what Lacan calls a "captivating image." We might think of the ways issues circulate as images indexing a psychotic atmosphere. Unending streams of photos of murdered children, snipers on top of university buildings, demolished cities, and so on can make us feel crazy. Why is this happening? Why doesn't anybody do anything? Images cover over the holes in meaning, the absence of a signifying structure in which common sense can be made. The psychotic adapts by fastening on the image, using it to get their bearings, within a dialectic of imaginary identification. Does the image mirror the ego back to itself or does it reflect an aggressor? Does one see oneself or one's rival? The captivating image doesn't offer a position from which to see oneself as a subject. Remaining at the level of the imaginary, it's an object within a relation characterized by identification, aggression, and rivalry. There's no third, symbolic, space or terrain of meaning.

"Psychosis" indexes the ways that people living in neofeudalizing times try to become subjects by creating meaning in the context of a war around meaning. Words mean different things to different people; everyone has their own definition. If one can identify with something, it matters. If one can't, then that something will likely be feared or hated. We feel threatened or aggressed by everything around us, fighting for survival in systems beyond our control. In his classic study of feudalism, Marc Bloch tells us that "behind all social life there was a background of the primitive, of submission to uncontrollable forces of unrelievable physical contrasts."[6] This background is neofeudalism's foreground: networked personalized media, extreme inequality, and climate change in a setting where nothing makes sense, where cruelty and violence run rampant while images, words, language, and grammar are weapons and terrain of battle.

In his illuminating exploration of ordinary psychosis, Darian Leader sets out the three types of psychosis recognized by the Lacanian field: paranoia, schizophrenia, and melancholia.[7] Paranoia is characterized by a sense of persecution. For the paranoiac, "It's always someone else's fault . . . The paranoiac is in the position of a complainant, pointing to the fault in the other."[8] As Leader makes clear, contemporary society is a habitat conducive to the flourishing of paranoia: not only are we enjoined to think of ourselves as victims, but we receive validation for detailing the trauma and injustice that we suffer. The paranoiac may strive to be an agent of change, opposing cruelty and corruption. Often paranoia manifests in an attachment to certainty, whether one found in the truths of ancient texts or in detailed and comprehensive knowledge of oppression. Again, the affective infrastructure of neofeudalizing society supports these attributes as it encourages everyone to do what they can to save the world and enjoins us to find out for ourselves the real truth behind the lies—even as there is no space where divergent truths are reconciled. To be sure, in a brutal, violent world there are real victims and there are good and true fighters against oppression. What we lack is agreement on who they are, perpetually suspicious of the Real of power and enjoyment. Who are the monsters and who are the heroes?

With schizophrenia, the other is not an external oppressor. The other is inside; the subject isn't separate from the other. My thoughts may be the thoughts of someone else. The schizophrenic isn't sure. Any message could mean anything, come from anywhere. The schizophrenic may not recognize their own body, wondering if it is someone else or experiencing it as a surface to which they have no real attachment.

Finally, the third type of psychosis, melancholia, involves self-blame: anything that's wrong is my fault. The melancholic repeats an endless litany of self-loathing, how useless and awful they are. Doom-scrolling confirms it.

The right is generally more likely to fall into paranoia and the left into melancholic self-hatred, but the terms *right* and *left* are unstable, most useful for those who want to say what they are not. Those who feel buffeted between the two—or by the relentless and ongoing effects of economic immiseration, climate catastrophe, and genocide in a setting where nobody cares—might fall into a sort of everyday schizophrenia, alienated from and punished by their own bodies, unable to shake tormenting and intrusive thoughts. Again, my claim is not that people are these sorts of subjects. It's that the affective atmosphere of neofeudalism is psychotic and these three types of psychosis—paranoia, schizophrenia, and melancholia—provide the patterns for imagining oneself and one's experience that the social manor encourages. Most people and political orientations resist easy categorization. As we're incessantly reminded, everyone is different, and nothing compares to anything.

Neofeudalism's psychotic anxieties pervade the fraught terrain of identity politics. For some, attachment to an identity provides grounding in a harsh, uncertain world. They can anchor their politics in their identity, speaking from their own experience as well as the experience of their people. For others, identity doesn't determine politics; politics determines identity. Their politics tells them who they are. When another challenges, criticizes, or rejects their politics, they experience it as a personal assault. In both instances, critique makes a space unsafe. It places in question the core of one's being.

We saw examples of the complex uncertainties disrupting identity politics and its reflexivization (politics determines identity) intensify around Jewish identity in the wake of the October 7, 2023, Al Aqsa Flood operation, Israel's and the US's subsequent genocide against the Palestinians, and the rise of the global movement for Palestinian liberation. Some Jewish

Americans experienced the attack on Israel as a deeply personal assault on their very existence. Other Jewish Americans led demonstrations calling for a ceasefire and denouncing Israel's indiscriminate use of force against civilians. Some non-Jews (such as US president Joe Biden) identified themselves as Zionists or criticized anti-Zionists for being anti-Semitic, even when the anti-Zionists were Jewish. Jewish identity was invoked as a ground for supporting and for condemning Israel, as a basis for joining as well as for fearing the encampments that swept US universities in April 2024.

For all its publicly demonstrated intensity, none of this was new. As Antony Lerman documents, Jewish people have been engaged in "an enormously hateful and bitter" debate over anti-Semitism and its relation to anti-Zionism and the critique of Israeli state policies since at least the 1970s. The debate "connects with, draws on and mutually reinforces deeper social, cultural and political fractures which characterize a world where 'post-truth,' 'fake news' and 'alternative facts' undermine the values of trust, integrity and critical discourse."[9] Barnaby Raine explicitly emphasizes the paranoia pervading "all sides now," anti-Semites, anti-anti-Semites, those who feel they might be threatened, and those skeptical of anything taking the focus off Palestine.[10]

Identity politics and its reflexivization collapse the signifier into the subject. Lacan famously said that the signifier represents the subject for another signifier. With the collapse of politics into identity, instead of the signifier taking the place of the subject, instead of the utterance running on its own momentum along a path determined by a chain of significations, there is just the person making the utterance. What they say matters less than who they are: friend or enemy? Instead of the question "Why are you telling me this?" there is only space for the question "Who are you?" We don't ask what people said. We only want to know who said it. *Who said it*? The answer allows us to perform millions of automatic classifying operations, turning our minds into ranking algorithms determining the status of the speaker, their worthiness to speak, the threat potential that they pose. If the wrong person says it, the statement, observation, or content is suspect. If the right person says it, then we agree in advance.

Both fastening politics on identity and identity on politics attempt to combat the decline of symbolic efficiency. They struggle on the imaginary plane in the ceaseless rivalry between me and the other. Words might be defined differently, but we can hold on to our own experiences, speak for ourselves, assert the commitments that define us "as a communist," "as a mother," "as an anti-imperialist." Absent shared meaning and references, we have nothing to turn to but ourselves, our experiences. We may not be psychotic in any individual pathological sense, but the atmosphere in which we try to think and breathe forces us into the paranoid, rivalrous struggle where someone is out to get us and we have no one to blame but ourselves, as the voices on our screens and in our heads never cease reminding us. Anxiety doesn't deceive.

The intensities around mental health, language, and even jokes attest to the extreme vulnerability of the subject unable to find place and protection in a chain of signifiers; anything I say is WHO I AM. My core. If you say something that is anything less than affirming, you have harmed me, dealt a blow. Sticks and stones may break my bones, but slogans will eradicate my very existence—rather like the side effects of Dylar in Don DeLillo's *White Noise*. In the novel, Dylar is an experimental drug for eliminating the fear of death. One of Dylar's side effects is collapsing the difference between signifier and signified. One person says "hail of bullets" and the other drops to the ground, terrified. I'm suggesting that the collapse between signifier and subject is even worse. The words of another harm me not because I can't tell the difference between words and objects but because I can't tell the difference between words and the person who utters them. Your disagreement denies my right to exist. When you say something I can't accept, you are trying to kill me. How could I ever feel safe knowing you are out there?

Nobody cares

We can distinguish two modalities of "nobody cares." The first requires a predicate, the designation of an object that nobody cares about. As soon as an object is named, though, the sentence becomes contradictory. Clearly, somebody cares—namely, the person worried that nobody else cares. Although I say "nobody cares," in saying this I am expressing that I care and that you should too. But instead of directly saying "I care, and you should too," the statement "nobody cares" exposes a lack that it occupies but cannot fill, because the lack can't be filled. I may care, but that's not enough. It's utterly inadequate to the endless care that is required. My inadequacy is exposed and displaced onto the absent subject supposed to care.

This first mode of "nobody cares" is moralizing; it's an expression of concern voiced as a judgment that carries an unstated command. It's shameful, outrageous, that nobody cares. An article in the *Jewish Chronicle* on the Gaza solidarity encampments quoted a third-year student named Julia: "No one cares . . . none of my friends who aren't Jewish have asked me how I'm doing."[11] The hearer or reader is hailed as someone who should feel the same way, who should join in the outrage. If they are interpellated by this hail, then they too will care. The moralizing modality is thus performative rather than constative. It doesn't describe a situation. It tries to change a situation, indirectly, by insinuating that one should care without straightforwardly demanding it. Voiced through a statement of absence, the "ought" dimension of the utterance is free-floating, amorphous.

What makes the interpellation effective is shame. I should care about Haiti and climate change and corruption and students' feelings not because any of these are my fault or are things that I can affect but because of the kind of person I am. Am I someone who cares or not? Am I a member of an ethical and social world that acknowledges deep interconnections and feels something when these interconnections are broken? If it stings to discover that I have not cared about something I should, then I will feel a sense of shame alleviated only by joining the community of those who care about X, the thing, the matter at hand. I assume the "ought" to avoid the shame. Communicative capitalism provides networked opportunities to perform this assumption: when I like and share and change my profile pic, I demonstrate to myself most of all that I am someone who cares. But assuming the ought won't be enough: that somebody cares doesn't negate "nobody cares"—it adds to it, intensifies it; now more people feel that nobody cares. Starting to care, being interpellated as caring, doesn't produce the subject supposed to care; it just expands the affective sense of incapacity engendered by its absence.

The second modality of "nobody cares" is reactive. Here someone says "nobody cares" in response to an initial statement of concern. As a response, it aims to deflect or unravel the concern: *the soup is too salty, I stumbled over my words, I had to miss the party, my hair looks terrible.* That nobody cares is a relief—whether comforting or indifferent, it says, *Forget about what is concerning you. You're free; there's no need to feel hemmed in by others' expectations.*

Whereas the first modality is binding, the second is liberating—from what? The first modality. The second doesn't simply express an obliviousness to social ties; it actively negates them. They aren't there. They don't hold, and to think that they do is to wrap yourself in an illusion that is harmful, that holds you back. An episode in US politics from May 2022 exemplifies the point. The then House minority leader Kevin McCarthy (a Republican) initially held Trump responsible for the January 6, 2021, assault on the Capitol. But given Trump's grip on the Republican Party, McCarthy backed down. He said that he never blamed Trump. The *New York Times* found a video where McCarthy explicitly blamed Trump. McCarthy continued to deny it—despite the video evidence. The Republican talking point on the matter was "nobody cares" (except the *New York Times*). Since Republicans view the *New York Times* as anti-Trump, its words don't matter, and nobody else cares. McCarthy and the rest of his party were liberated from any expectation of consistency or accountability which their words would generate. There are no ties that bind. Nobody cares. Similarly, in the UK Conservative members of Parliament didn't care that the prime minister had a party while the rest of the country was stuck in lockdown. They too were shameless in their liberation from the expectation that words have binding power: they had the privilege not to care. The non-duped win. Melania Trump expressed a variation on the same theme in October 2018: at a visit to a shelter in Texas in which migrant children were being detained, she wore a jacket that said, "I don't really care, do you?" She later explained that the message was meant for left-wing bullies in the media, a way to tell them that she didn't care what they said about her. Their words didn't matter; she would go on doing what she thought was right.[12] The binding and liberating modalities of "nobody cares" presuppose the same subject, the absent subject supposed to care.

Lacan describes the process of transference in the course of psychoanalysis via the *subject supposed to know*. The analysand is stimulated to talk in analysis because she assumes that the analyst knows what's up with her, the secret of her desire, what it all means, how to cure her symptoms or end her suffering. The subject supposed to know is a premise of the analytic relationship.

Žižek presents the *subject supposed to believe* as a constitutive feature of the symbolic order, a way to understand the trust that institutionality presupposes. In contrast to the exceptional quality of the analytic relation and its basis in a subject supposed to know, the everyday operation of the symbolic order relies on the displaced supposition of an other who believes. Santa Claus is an easy example: people go through the motions for the sake of the children who believe in him. These motions produce the spirit of Christmas as their effect. The humor of Christmas movies is often that the children know full well that Santa isn't real; they pretend to believe for the sake of their parents.

Education and legality likewise presuppose others who believe in them. For many faculty, part of the undermining effect of moving courses onto Zoom during the pandemic was the confrontation with rows of black boxes denoting the absolute minimal degree of engagement with a lecture. That minimum wasn't enough to support a belief that we were teaching. Prerecorded lectures are even worse. Now in addition to unread readings we give unheard lectures to an app. More to the point, the institutionality of education presupposes others who believe in it: the employers who value degrees, the accreditation boards who attest to standards, the alumni and graduates who validate their experience, repeating the names of their alma maters with appreciation. Education matters to those who believe it's important.

Legality is more than force. It extends beyond the activities of police via practices through which police can be believed to be different from armed vigilantes and criminals. The passive expression "can be believed" points to the subject supposed to believe. There doesn't have to be an actual person who believes; in fact, such a person often appears naïve. Belief is displaced and deferred, posited as a basic condition.[13] Someone, somewhere believes that a badge and a uniform indicate that their bearers are authorized to stop cars, search our homes, carry weapons, and issue orders. Someone, somewhere, believes vaccines are safe, money is an acceptable means of exchange, the election was fair, the monarchy makes sense, and so on. Trust, credibility, and a minimal degree of charity characterize institutionality as such.

University presidents and administrators went far in undermining belief in education and legality in April 2024 as they called police to their campuses to tear down their students' Gaza solidarity encampments. Columbia University led the way, not only because president Minouche Shafik's congressional testimony undermined basic assumptions of academic freedom by pandering to Republican Representative Elise Stefanik's aggressive and narrow-minded questioning, but because Shafik's decision to call in hundreds of police, brutally arrest hundreds of students, disregard faculty governance procedures, move all classes to Zoom, and cancel graduation revealed the university no longer to be a place for thinking and learning. It was a walled fortress devoid of students and faculty, nothing but real estate and police in the service of big donors. On April 30, 2024, UCLA did its part as police stood by while masked counter-protestors violently attacked students at their peaceful encampment. The counter-protestors sprayed chemicals at the students, shot fireworks into their encampments, and swung at them with poles and boards. Some wore clothes featuring pro-Israel slogans and blared a song about the military campaign against Gaza.[14] Others were recognizable figures from California's far right, having been active in the anti-trans and anti-vaccine movements and photographed making Nazi salutes.[15] When the police arrived at UCLA, the counter-protestors cheered, "USA! USA! USA!"[16]

The more we doubt that there is a subject who believes, the more we hear and see others act in ways that contradict what we thought we all accepted to be true about social norms and institutions, the more fragmented and unstable the symbolic order becomes. The subject supposed to believe can't fulfill its symbolic function. Our experience today is of multiple, contradictory, incompatible beliefs. Different communities believe different things; what makes them different communities are the different beliefs that tie them together. Some today, such as those who attack LGBTQ people in the name of the traditional family or those who insist on buttressing a specific Judeo-Christian vision of culture and society, attempt to shore up a unity that was always a myth. Others on social media and in the neoliberal university urge us to care about different beliefs and experiences, but not too much. Everyone is entitled to their own opinion (except about Palestine), and we are wrong to think and speak otherwise. When the symbolic order is functioning, people typically suppress their knowledge of its founding and ongoing violence. Heroic origin stories, rituals, progress narratives, and so on cover over systemic violence. Under conditions where the symbolic is fragmented and declining, the underlying violence can no longer be denied; it's felt, overwhelming, threatening, and exhausting. The system is nothing but misogynist, racist, settler colonialist, fascistic, exploitative, and oppressive. Nobody cares.

Nobody cares because care can't register. There is no big Other who could care in a setting where the subject supposed to believe is already fragmented, pluralized, multiple. Small others can care, but multiple small others don't add up to a big one. The big Other requires a change in register, the abstract symbolic level of representation. Practical activities of caring, circulating statements of care, don't generate the subject supposed to care; this subject only appears as missing, in statements of a generalized incapacity. Individuated and small group activities don't compensate for the absence; they respond to and mark it—we wouldn't be having to do all this if somebody cared. For example, the typical neoliberal response to any problem that arises in the general setting of communicative capitalism is demanding transparency, providing more information, publishing a list, displaying ingredients, holding workshops or trainings. All such measures deflect and disperse responsibility from a central agent or subject. It's up to the individual who cares to do with them what she will.

The social manor

Let's return to the two modalities of "nobody cares," the moralistic and the liberating, the binding and the freeing, the stinging and the soothing. Since they index the absence of the big Other, these modes operate in a field where the imaginary and the Real blur together, where there is no symbolic transcendence, no third place from which conflict is resolved. The modalities operate on the plane of the imaginary, amid relations of fear, rivalry, and aggression. The statement "nobody cares" can be an attack, an attempt to dominate others by asserting a particular concern as primary. Even mentioning something else that should be cared for can be taken as an aggressive affront, an instance of illegitimate "whataboutism." In its liberating mode, "nobody cares" may be dismissive, abandoning: stop complaining, stop making excuses, stop asserting yourself and your issues, you don't matter. It's no wonder that politics collapses into conflicts about language, the meanings of words, what can and cannot be said, and who decides. Absent the protection of the signifier, statements directly reflect the power of the one who makes them. Their content matters less than the wealth or prestige of their utterer, which has different degrees of force in different contexts. The speaker trumps the spoken. Strength comes from recognizing that any force words have is the effect of a social convention; to be free of that convention, all that's necessary is recognizing that any bond is personal, local, a matter of the specific ties accepted in one's own group. When the political is personal, struggles erupt over privilege and servility, who can get away with what and who has to bend the knee.

Without criticism or irony, the Nobel Prize–winning economist Paul Krugman observed that billionaires "command deference, even servility, from those who depend on their largess."[17] He cautions that commanding deference may not be a particularly smart move, since people will tell billionaires what they want to hear. It could even be dangerous if it leads to political alliance with authoritarians willing to run roughshod over the rule of law. Yet Krugman's warning seems tone deaf in the context of commanded servility, of personal ties of dependence born of extreme inequality. Notice: the relation of servility he evokes is not an employment relation; it's a dependent relation.

Marc Bloch reminds us that "the feudal system meant the rigorous economic subjection of a host of humble folks to a few powerful men."[18] Krugman appeals to liberal norms in a neofeudal setting; government by men has already supplanted government by law. Rather than abstract law applying equally to each and all, expectations and obligations are differentiated in terms of one's place in hierarchical networks of privilege. The powerful expect loyalty from their dependents. Those lower on the food chain fawn over, cater to, and serve the interests of their betters, hoping if not to rise than at least for a little protection from the worst of a fall. The rule of law has already crumbled: privilege is the knowledge that one doesn't have to play by common rules. The substitution of personalized ties for the abstract and general relations associated with bourgeois modernity imbues the present with its neofeudal structure of feeling. Bloch's description of links in a hierarchical chain joining great and small evokes our own hierarchized networks. Struggles around privilege and status, perpetually refought, never won, replace any sense of guaranteed rights. There's no resolution.

Hegel's famous figure of the lord and bondsman, dialectically reversing the one into the other, helps illuminate these affective dimensions of the neofeudal social manor. Drawing out the multiple references to the struggle between the lord and bondsman throughout Hegel's work, Andrew Cole insists on its fundamentally feudal dialectic. The struggle personifies a primary conflict in feudal society: the conflict over possession. To work or use the land didn't mean one owned it. Owning wasn't sufficient for benefiting from land, and title depended on personal hierarchical relations of fealty and protection. Hegel explains in his lectures on the philosophy of history:

> The feudal lords or great barons enjoyed, properly speaking, no free or absolute possession, any more than their dependents; they had unlimited power of the latter, but at the same time they also were vassals of princes higher and mightier than themselves, and to whom they were engagements— which, it must be confessed, they did not fulfil [sic] except under compulsion.[19]

Not only does the struggle over possession occur within a personal hierarchical relation, but it is inseparable from a broader network of coercive and protective relations. No one is independent. Everyone depends on someone for something, which makes them vulnerable by putting them at permanent risk of domination or annihilation.

In "Seminar III," Lacan uses the struggle between the lord and bondsman to explain the order of the imaginary. Lacan follows his teacher Alexandre Kojève in using the terms *master* and *slave* and in conceiving the struggle as a matter of autonomy and recognition. The struggle is fought over an object, a thing (Cole emphasizes that the thing is land). Lord and bondsman each desire the thing because the other desires it. What's at stake for Lacan, then, is a primary rivalry fought out via the thing. He tells the story as a tale of the lord's idiocy: "It was in no way the object of enjoyment that was at issue, but rivalry as such."[20] The lord wants the bondsman's recognition, but the recognition of a bondsman is worthless. So even though the master gets to enjoy the thing, he doesn't get what he really wanted. For Lacan, this primitive competition is overcome in speech: "Speech is always a pact, an agreement, people get one with one another, they agree—this is yours, this is mine, this is this, that is that."[21] Without agreement in speech, without the pact, the rivalry continues, and with it the possibility of annulling or being annulled.

Cole's emphasis on the feudal dialectic suggests a version of the pact where matters are not so simple. The rivalry continues. Something might be sort of yours and sort of mine, and it will all depend on who has the strength and the will to make it so. What the lord really wants is the recognition of a higher lord, a prince granting him title to some land. But even that won't be enough, because without bondsmen of his own to work the land the lord can't enjoy it, and even with bondsmen of his own he can at any moment be called upon to perform loyalty obligations associated with vassalage. Pacts thus function like little objects circulating within a setting of networked struggles rather than as ways to resolve them. Lots of little pacts don't add up to a big one. Agreement in speech isn't enough to resolve much of anything for very long.

In his close reading of Hegel and Lacan, Mladen Dolar shows how lordship is effectively the fantasy of the bondsman. Dolar writes, "If lordship is a symbolic relation—not something based on external repression—then fantasy is the way that this relation can be actual for the subject, the minimal part of 'illusion necessary for domination.'"[22] If lordship is *not* a symbolic relation, if it *is* something based on external repression, then domination doesn't need to be accompanied by illusion. That lords are vassals means that they have been compelled to agree; they've been forced to accept a protective arrangement with a king or higher lord. Compulsion goes all the way down through the pacts linking high and low. Submission is provisional.

Lacan considers psychosis in terms of the imaginary dialectic:

> For want of being able in any way to re-establish his pact with the other, for want of being able to make any symbolic mediation whatsoever between what is new and himself, the subject moves into another mode of mediation, completely different from the former, and substitutes for symbolic mediation a profusion, an imaginary proliferation, into which the central signal of a possible mediation is introduced in a deformed and profoundly asymbolic fashion.[23]

Absent the mediation of the symbolic, the subject is confined to the imaginary. Here everything is fragmented and multiplied, "decomposed into a multitude of imaginary beings."[24] Decomposition is parcellization at the level of the subject. It doesn't usher in a new kind of psychic freedom but rather the intrusion of ever more aggressive rivalries, ever more threats and suspicions of threats.

Consider some examples. An academic institution puts together a Gender Inclusiveness Task Force for Data Management. One of its goals is updating the forms the institution uses to collect data. A premise behind the task force's work is that "asking a person about their identity in a manner that is based on best practices can help people feel seen and included." The grammar of the sentence implies that people who ask the questions feel seen and included. The sentence doesn't say anything about the people answering questions. The slippage suggests an imaginary identification mediated by the form people are instructed to fill out: *I feel seen and included when I ask questions about gender and the form does this for me.* The form includes separate categories for gender identity, pronouns, legal sex, and sexual orientation.

There are multiple options within each category, including "prefer not to answer" and "not listed above." The gender identity, pronouns, and sexual orientation categories each include seven options in addition to "prefer not to answer" and "not listed above." Does the multiplication of categories on a form turn the form into an object capable of communicating respect or even care? The demand is overwhelming, so many categories to consider, so many possibilities of misrecognizing oneself, possibilities the form simultaneously avows and denies with its profusion of options. How will the answers be used? For whose enjoyment are they provided? In addition to triggering anxiety, the form might elicit a paranoid response: What business is this of yours? Why is someone trying to pin me down?

Another example: elections. Typically, we think of elections in terms of going to vote and then hearing the outcome. In the US, as elections have become more fraught, we learn more about the details: voting machines that may or may not work, bags of ballots, blank ballots, local election officials, state officials who oversee recounts, legal proceedings involving what and how recounts are carried out, political struggles over who has the right to certify or challenge election results. Once the process is decomposed into its elements, its legitimacy appears more uncertain. It's easier to see where things can go wrong, where people can insert their interests, how power and privilege enter the picture. It's harder to see how the pieces cohere into a whole. What were ritualized processes of social order appear rotten, stained by private enjoyment and everyday realities of breakdown and dysfunction. There's no big Other of the symbolic, only rivalrous little others circulating through their networks of dependency.

In his seminar on anxiety, Lacan writes, "If what we're dealing with is too much, then you're not lacking it."[25] The subject supposed to care is missing, but this missing doesn't register as lack. What registers are the inescapable demands and unavoidable enjoyment of the Other. We can't find a space safe from the excesses drowning, suffocating, obliterating us. It's all too much, even when it's not enough.

The subject who cares

Many on the left think of sovereignty as the enemy (Antonio Negri is a proponent of this view). The truth is that fragmentation indicates the absence of the universal, the loss of that symbolic location from which we can make sense of the world and achieve a bit of respite from anxiety, rivalry, and aggression. Fragmentation—the collapse of the symbolic and the parcellization of sovereignty—makes it inaccurate to posit a specifically neofeudal subject. But we can recognize its absence, tracking the effects of this absence in our psychotic affective landscape. When all ties are personal, the stronger—whether in wealth, prestige, or shamelessness—prevail. People become motivated by their proximity to strength, like so many vassals courting favor from lord and king. Service isn't valued as care; it's associated with servility as deference is expected and inscribed at every turn. Knowing who your betters are is effected through an epistemology of pain—and we never know when or from where another blow will strike.

Lacan says that "anxiety is only ever surmounted when the Other has been named."[26] He is talking about love, transference, and the desire of the analyst, but we can glimpse political possibility here in his evocation of a kind of structuring guidance, a relation to a place or position that cuts through the demands and enjoyment absorbing us. To name the Other means to put in place a structure through which one can make sense of the world and one's place in it.[27] This is never a purely individual endeavor. Analysis can't be done alone (Lacan takes issue with Freud's attempt at self-analysis). It requires the presence of another who can help us separate ourselves from what torments us. The analyst is irreducible to the individuality of a person; their listening is informed by a discipline, by a teaching, practice, and institution.

In left politics, this is the place of the communist party.[28] The party provides an affective structure counter to the catastrophic anxiety pervading neofeudalism. It organizes the transferential space of the subject supposed to know as the knowledge of a collective political subject. Like the knowledge of the clinic, the knowledge of the party arises over time, in struggle. Like the discipline of analysis, the discipline of the party is a matter of practice, a necessary condition for practical action.

One of the ways that the party provides relief from anxiety is through its line. Rather than endless multiplicity, the party provides direction. Clarifying expectations and establishing boundaries, the party installs for its members a symbolic order that recomposes the decomposed proliferation of the imaginary. Another way to express the same point: through the party, the members establish these expectations for themselves. The party is the form enabling this establishment, this expression of common acceptance of shared expectations. One need not be blown about by neofeudalism's prevailing winds; one can be steadfast in knowing for what and with whom one stands. In a setting of rivalry and aggression, we know which side we are on. We have comrades who have our backs.[29] We don't go into political struggle unarmed and alone. Our steadfastness doesn't come from certainty (it isn't psychotic); it comes from shared and practical belief in the party as a necessary form for the political struggle for communism. The party will err; it isn't an omnipotent big Other. That it will err doesn't mean we don't need it: the party is the form through which learning and redress is possible.

Neofeudalism and its paranoias and anxieties are not inescapable. Common and collective practice opens up a way out.

With the party, one is no longer the object of the unbearable demands of an inescapable other. One becomes part of the subject who believes in the possibility of communism, the subject who cares.

Conclusion: The Servant Vanguard

Capitalism isn't immortal—although from time to time it's depicted as undead. It had a beginning, and it will have an end. The beginning of this mode of production lasted several centuries—and was a violent, bloody process inextricable from colonialism and slavery. Its ending appears to be approaching more quickly if no less violently: hoarding, predation, and destruction are replacing competition, investment, and improvement as primary drivers of wealth accumulation. In the 1970s and '80s, we were told that information technology and services would expand the number of white-collar jobs, value creative and highly educated labor, and result in growth and prosperity for all. An advanced capitalist knowledge economy would replace industrial commodity production. That's not quite the way it turned out. Deindustrialization and deagrarianization led to a global rise in services, but the vast majority are unwaged, low paid, informal, and precarious.

The array of services is broad, from the financial, legal, real estate, and insurance services associated with the much-maligned professional-managerial class to the cleaners, security guards, delivery drivers, and home health aides struggling to bring home enough to cover endlessly increasing rent. In much of this "stagnant sector," growth is slow, dependent more on suppressing wages and pushing workers than on technological innovation.[1] With the bulk of jobs consisting of low-skill, low-productivity personal services, inequality intensifies, the many locked into serving the few. Most of us are minions now, proletarianized neoserfs tethered to the phones, apps, platforms, and personal connections we need to access basic means of subsistence. The few use their political and economic power to seize ever larger portions of the proceeds of labor, evading public law while subjecting us to their private dominion. We are exploited through the wage that is further expropriated from us via ever-increasing rents, fines, charges, and fees.

The Marxist hope was that capital was digging its own grave by building up massive means of production. Not only would industrialization end scarcity, provide abundance, and enable us to meet social needs, but the concentration of workers in central locations would generate the class consciousness necessary for rising up against and defeating the owners of capital. Even more, liberal democracy—the legal and political system developed by the bourgeoisie to protect their interests— would help the proletariat develop the political skills necessary for struggle and victory. While Marxists have always disagreed on the extent to which participation in bourgeois democratic parliamentary politics could lead to socialism, few have discounted the importance of literacy, voting rights, political participation, and party formation to the development of proletarian political consciousness. By burying capitalism, the working class would make real for everyone the promises of freedom, equality, and justice that the liberal bourgeoisie had reserved for owners of property.

Forty years of neoliberalism have undermined these ideals. A harsh winner-take-all economy eviscerated the social-democratic welfare state. Health, education, green space, clean air, and clean water are still available—as private goods for those who can pay for them. The same holds for justice. Able to retain armies of lobbyists and attorneys to fight their battles, the rich evade responsibility. The laws subjecting the many to surveillance, harassment, debt, and fines don't apply to them. It's no wonder that disproportionality, disparity, and privilege have become primary terms in the contemporary language of grievance and redress. Someone is always ahead of us, getting more than they deserve, more than their share. What can equality even mean in a society of nuanced hierarchical gradations? Equal to what? In the US, this is what democracy looks like—stolen elections, politically indistinguishable candidates, and the static outrage of a civil war, where, as in Thucydides's description in his history of the Peloponnesian War, words have changed their ordinary meanings. Free markets and free speech have devolved into communicative capitalism's subjection of communication to the logic of market competition: circulation value displaces use value, and platform owners determine what circulates. Freedom has become dependence, all that has melted into air a fetter more solid than iron.

Living the transition from capitalism to neofeudalism, we have to be attuned to overlapping forms and contradictory logics, to the ways that the same processes fit within fundamentally different modes of production and accumulation. Such attunement is disserved by the localism and anti-statism uniting communitarians and libertarians left and right. Sovereignty isn't the problem; ours is an age of suzerainty where deals between the powerful easily override even the smallest popular victories. Privatized jurisprudence, fragmentation into zones, and tech companies more powerful than most state governments alert us to parcellated sovereignty's new conditions of struggle: impersonal conditions of perpetually displaced accountability wherein personal power thrives. Social and ecological reproduction crises in the hinterlands— hinterlands perforating as well as surrounding thriving cityscapes—and the psychotic atmosphere of anxiety, rivalry, and aggression reveal the class conflict characteristic of the social manor. No longer confined within the hidden abode of production, it pervades consumption and circulation as ever-multiplying fees and fines prey on our lives and futures.

The sector of servants doesn't feel like what we've been told class should feel like. Where is the solidarity? Instead of finding safety in numbers, we are left to go it alone, fighting our own battles not to get ahead but just to survive. Nearly all servants have to sell their labor power to survive—not all, since some of the lawyers and hedge fund managers have hoards sufficient to retire in luxury—but we hold on to status differences for dear life. Our labor power sells below its value. With brands as our sigils, we construct new ones as influencers, frequent fliers, and preferred customers with elite status and VIP access to the most exclusive restaurants, lounges, and hotels. Just as proximity to the lord or king mattered in a feudal age, so do gradations in fame and privilege preoccupy those who no longer see equality as a measure of justice.

This is a grim picture. Fortunately, it's not inevitable. My story of the neofeudalizing tendencies in contemporary capitalism describes the way things will proceed if we don't develop the political will and capacity to push in a communist direction. I conclude by considering ideas on the left that reinforce neofeudalism and locating possibilities for combatting it. We aren't doomed to being buried alive in capital's grave. The sector of servants contains a vanguard that can lead the way out of it.

Beyond subsistence

In the late 1990s and early 2000s, scholar-activists did significant work documenting the impact of neoliberal globalization. Attentive to the ravaging of communities around the world, they theorized debt, enclosure, accumulation by dispossession, planetary urbanization, and the rise of global cities. Some of those working in and influenced by the Italian tradition of autonomous Marxism found a positive alternative to neoliberal globalization in the commons, a generative political and social space separate from the public sphere of the state and the private sphere of family and market. Silvia Federici's contribution was especially influential as it brought out the gendered dimensions of neoliberal privatization and developed the idea of commoning as a political and economic practice for generating cooperative social relations. Yet even as her analyses drew crucial attention to the unwaged work of social reproduction and helped keep alive a vital counterdiscourse to the hegemonic capitalist one, in retrospect its limits are apparent: Federici assumes rather than contests a neofeudal order. More precisely, Federici's account of social reproduction, critique of Marx, and rejection of the state reflect an embrace of pre-capitalist economic and political relations generally associated with feudalism.

First, influenced by Mariarosa Dalla Costa and Selma James and developed in the course of the Wages for Housework Campaign, Federici's analysis of social reproduction emphasizes the productivity of women's unwaged domestic labor. While Federici concedes that housework was minimal in nineteenth-century working-class homes, she nonetheless repeatedly attacks Marx for ignoring it. He ignores it, she says, because he fails to see it as value-producing labor. Federici is fully aware of the definitions Marx gives to the terms through which he analyzes capitalism. *Value* refers to exchange value; it designates a quantitative relation between different products of labor. What enables different products of labor to be brought into relation, to be compared and exchanged, is what they have in common—namely, labor time. Labor time doesn't refer to how long it takes a particular person to make a particular thing. It refers to an aggregate, to the amount of time it takes workers in general to make commodities, what Marx calls socially necessary labor time. The development of manufacturing and industry dramatically decreased the amount of labor time necessary to make virtually every item we encounter in everyday life. They also led to an explosion of new and combined industrial and technological processes and to the production of things few of us would have ever imagined we could possibly need. Federici understands all this, but she asserts that Marx neglects the production of the most important commodity of all: labor power. She acknowledges the justified critique of this move: "Women produce living individuals—children, relatives, friends—not labor power."[2] But she does so only to dismiss it: just as labor power "can only exist in the living individual," so is it "equally impossible to draw a line between the two corresponding aspects of reproductive work"—that is, the reproduction of the person and of labor power.[3] The human is collapsed into labor.

The primary problem with Federici's approach to reproductive labor lies in her treatment of value. That work is necessary doesn't mean it's productive; it doesn't mean that it produces exchange value. To produce the bearer of labor power is not the same as producing labor power, just as producing the bearer of clothes is not the same as producing clothes. Treating women's reproductive work as analogous to commodity production—that is, as productive of abstract interchangeable units—misconstrues the character of domestic labor, in effect providing a new variation on the commodity fetishism Marx so famously theorized: relations between people take on the character of relations between things. Speaking of "the production of human beings" concedes alienation in advance. Where we might find joy, we discover cogs. Although in English we use the word *labor* as synonymous with giving birth, we shouldn't confuse sexual reproduction with commodity production. When we have children, we aren't simply producing a labor force for capitalism. We are bringing new possibilities into the world, people who may fight back and change everything. No Beanie Baby™ ever did that.

Had she acknowledged that caring for others involves necessary but unproductive labor, Federici might have been able to theorize the way the rise of services opens up a path out of capitalism. The household is not a capitalist enterprise organized on the basis of capitalist laws of motion. Neither is the issue women's unwaged labor in the home: for millennia poor and enslaved women have nursed the children, bathed the bodies, and scrubbed the floors of the better off; for centuries the household has been a site of waged as well as unwaged labor. What matters today is that capitalism's reliance on services is contributing to its becoming neofeudal. Precisely because care and reproduction can't be fully technologized, precisely because technological development results in an ever-larger sector of servants, precisely because caring for people comes up against real limits with respect to "efficiency" (nurses can care only for a limited number of patients, for example), a society of servants cannot be a capitalist society. Services require that we think in terms of their use value, not their exchange value.

That services have expanded takes us a step toward approaching the economy with an emphasis on meeting social needs not making profits. It's no accident that all over the world teachers, nurses, and other service workers have been at the vanguard of the new class struggle. The struggle around social reproduction is real, and it's real because it's about so much more than housework; it's about securing the basic conditions for social and ecological life. As more work has become directed to securing these conditions, and as it remains ill-paid and disconnected from capital accumulation, the ability of service workers to fight back has increased—and will increase.

There is nothing world-historical about housework. It's part of a realm of necessity rather than freedom. The household doesn't produce great inventions; changes in everyday practice in one spot don't lead to or engender changes elsewhere. For the most part, the work remains roughly the same. Technological developments that result in the production of new commodities can make some tasks easier. Pressures on households to participate in waged labor can make most tasks harder. Roughly speaking, it's under feudal relations that the household appeared as a site of historical significance: arranged marriages, blood alliances, and court intrigue. Here the personal really was political.

Second, Federici's critique of Marx centers on her rejection of the idea that there is a progressive dimension to capitalism.[4] Contra Marx, she argues that capitalism has not created a basis for building communism.[5] Instead of leading to abundance, it has increased scarcity. Instead of engendering cooperation, it has inscribed difference.[6] And instead of inciting a revolutionary and victorious proletariat, it has confronted militant Indigenous and peasant movements. Federici's argument is one sided. Marx insisted on the dialectical character of capitalism. Enormous advances in productive capacity were accompanied by immense deprivation. Cooperation was always interwoven with competition. The victory of the working class was never guaranteed; it always depended on political struggle. The Marxist-Leninist tradition is anchored in this fact, committed to building alliances of workers and peasants, as well as to anti-colonial and anti-imperialist struggle. To present Marxism as nothing but a theory of the industrial working class misrepresents the whole of the twentieth century.

Federici rightly observes that there were large-scale forms of production and exchange prior to capitalism. She should acknowledge, though, how these depended on indebted, enslaved, enserfed, conscripted, imprisoned, and coerced labor. Neither the oppression of workers nor waged labor is original to capitalism. Federici is misleading when she says that "capitalism destroyed a society of the commons materially grounded not only in the collective use of land and collective work relations but in the daily struggle against feudal power, which created new cooperative forms of life."[7] The destruction of the commons was a process internal to feudalism that capitalists turned to their advantage. [8] Federici is mistaken when she claims that Marx "failed to see the that the coexistence of different labor regimes would remain an essential component of capitalist production."[9] Marx explicitly describes and documents the rise of a servant class—"modern domestic slaves"—as a consequence of "capitalist exploitation of machinery."[10]

One-sided portrayals of capitalism do real harm to contemporary left struggles. The idea that capitalism is purely regressive, that pre-capitalist societies were preferable, requires us to think that we would be better off struggling to survive in subsistence economies. We would have to adopt the conceit that penicillin, radios, and electrification are evidence of decline. Not one of us who reads and writes today can seriously pretend that our lives would have been much improved had we been born in the thirteenth century, especially if we are women. I would have died giving birth to my first child (had I survived the measles, mumps, and meningitis I contracted as a kid). Would I have time to write if I had to make clothes for myself and my children? If I had to gather wood and water every day? Denying any progressive features to capitalism traps us in a pastoral feudal fantasy belied by the multiplicity of everyday benefits that capitalist industrialization has provided and of which millions are still deprived. That the devastating environmental and human costs of capitalism are accompanied by things we actually like and have come to need is one of the challenges facing anti-capitalist organizing. To say this does not dispute the importance of agricultural and pastoral ways of life. Rather, it recognizes the reality of planetary urbanization as well as the real hardships facing agriculturalists and pastoralists on a warming planet. Droughts, fires, floods, excessive heat, excessive rain, disrupted weather patterns—these impact those working closely with nature most of all.

Federici's critique posits a productivist, Promethean version of Marx: industry and technology will save us all; "freedom comes through the machine."[11] Again, this is one sided. Perhaps more than anyone else, Marx recognized capitalism's destructive power. The capitalist development of industry has negative consequences for nature as well as workers, the degradation of the conditions of the soil and of working-class life.[12] Overturning capitalism will transform these relations, replacing capitalist compulsion with communist planning and administration. Whereas Federici takes the view that "capitalist industry, science, and technology" cannot be taken over and put to communist use, Marx thinks that associated producers can "govern the human metabolism with nature in a rational way, bringing it under their collective control instead of being dominated by it as a blind power, accomplishing it with the least expenditure of energy and in conditions most worthy and appropriate for their human nature."[13] People together—especially workers most familiar with the instruments and processes of labor—can rethink and repurpose the technologies around us. We can assess the dangers they present, consider how these might be mitigated, and then experiment, rank, and choose.

Industry and technology developed under capitalist conditions in the interest of capital as a class. These conditions are necessarily conditions of class struggle; working-class power itself affects the shape capitalism takes. Capital's endeavors to increase surplus labor time push it into a contradictory situation: it ends up reducing necessary labor time—that is, engendering the conditions where we are free to do much more than work.[14] To think that machinery, technology, and industry can free up labor time and enable us to spend more time doing what we will and to imagine a world where we can evaluate, discuss, and determine which machinery, technology, and industry best support the flourishing of people and the planet is hardly "technologistic." When she suggests that it is, Federici posits a neofeudal horizon where the negation of capitalism is a return to subsistence farming, artisanal labor, and small communities.

Finally, for decades Federici's thought and activism have highlighted developments now discernible as neofeudalizing. Her work brings out deagrarianization's separation of producers from their means of subsistence and workers' dependence on waged work that they are unable to access.[15] Especially attentive to the impact of IMF and World Bank policies on the Global South, she emphasizes the massive scale of land privatization, development of free-trade zones, and dismantling of welfare-state provisions associated with neoliberal globalization. Across all these, Federici tracks the "permanent reproduction crisis" that capitalism fosters.[16] And yet her solutions remain confined to adaptation and resistance, to insisting on the ongoing significance of community-building subsistence work. Why not seize the state, abolish private property, and make social reproduction—the thriving of people and the planet—the purpose of all national and international planning? While Federici's reports on women's land struggles around the world demonstrate people's refusal to accept the neocolonial "development" projects forced on them, her underlying political presuppositions are neofeudal. Rejecting a politics that targets the state, she focuses on community and the commons—that is, on fragmented, small-scale, local, face-to-face relations tied to reproductive labor. The house is to be reclaimed "as a center of collective life."[17] The unhoused and migrating don't fit in this vision, and it's difficult to see how apartment dwellers facing evictions might enact such a politics. This may be why the tenants' union is a popular organizing model in today's housing struggles; it enables tenants to build the power necessary to come up against landlords and win.

Federici's emphases on urban gardening and "pooling our resources" affirm approaches to mutual aid prominent today. They point to how connecting with others in common voluntary work can help end the anxiety and isolation pervading contemporary life. Nevertheless, these approaches remain exclusive, reactive, and limited in their ability to change the conditions out of which they emerge. They remain exclusive because the ideal of community presupposes the connections it aims to build, as if people facing disaster and deprivation necessarily or automatically see themselves and their interests as aligned and can maintain this alignment over the long haul. If that were true, wouldn't we see entire regions, countries, and cities already communizing themselves? Wouldn't the hinterlands be thriving precisely because they've been abandoned by capital? The approaches Federici celebrates remain reactive because they don't aim to defeat capitalism and its state. Even as she critiques the dismantling of the social welfare state, Federici doesn't call for its rebuilding or for the reformation of its provisions in a new international communist form. Finally, the approaches Federici considers remain limited because the horizon is confined to subsistence conditions on a planet that is making subsistence survival impossible. We can't expect urban gardens and small-scale agriculture to feed 8 billion people so long as the fossil fuel sector continues to drill and temperatures continue to rise. An organized anti-imperialist struggle against the system destroying people and the planet is the only plausible way out of the chronic crisis of social reproduction.

A neofeudal left

As my discussion of Federici demonstrates, prominent ideas on the contemporary left remain trapped in a neofeudal imaginary. For decades, leftists have echoed neoliberals with their critiques of centralism, sovereignty, and the state. Localism affirms parcellization, as if fragmentation into zones weren't a primary way capitalism is shielding itself from popular sovereignty. Emphases on subsistence and survival proceed as if peasant economies were plausible not only for that half of the planet that lives in cities (including 82 percent of North Americans and 74 percent of Europeans) but also for the millions displaced by climate change, war, and commercial land theft. The problem for most people dwelling in the hinterlands is that their political, social, and economic conditions are such that they can't make a living through agriculture (approximately fifty countries are classified as low-income food-deficit countries; most will bear the initial brunt of the changing climate; most are in Africa). They are caught up in capitalism such that they can't subsist outside it. Universal basic income is a similarly untenable survivalist approach.[18] It promises just enough to keep those in the hinterlands going—so long as they remain outside the cities where they can't afford to live. The fourth element of neofeudalism, catastrophic anxiety, appears in preoccupations with extinction and the end of the world, as if the next hundred years or so just don't matter.

These popular left positions suggest a future of small groups and communes engaged in subsistence farming and the production of artisanal cheese, perhaps on the edges of cities where survivalist enclaves rely on urban gardens and drone-wielding tech workers experiment with synthetic meat. Such groupings reproduce their lives in common, yet the commons they reproduce is necessarily small, local, and in some sense exclusive and elite—exclusive insofar as their numbers are necessarily limited; elite because the aspirations are culturally specific, tied to a scene and an ethos rather than a political orientation for a complex society. The future looks like cool cities surrounded by organic farms (with little attention to agricultural labor processes). Did the farmers choose to be farmers or were they born that way? Do they own their land? Share it? Work it for their tech overlords? Do they export their products? And what about the hidden conditions that make the cool cities possible—the builders, cleaners, and maintainers of infrastructure, the providers of transportation and communication, the carers for health, education, and children? Are the cities cool for them?

Popular left ideas converge in a fantasy where the idealization of peasant agriculture obscures the abandonment of hinterlands, rural areas, and cities that have been left behind while accentuating those elements of the urban that benefit the rich and educated—our robot future. High and low tech—ostensibly representative of competing left imaginaries—are two sides of the same neofeudal coin, new lords and serfs. Far from a vision anchored in the emancipation of the working class, the model can't see a working class—even when it's right before our eyes as the service sector supporting every aspect of contemporary life. Instead, left enthusiasm for robots and urban gardens gives us a vision that boils down to a wealthy fortress surrounded by a combination of farms and wastelands.

When work is imagined—and some on the left think that we should adopt a "post-work imaginary"—it looks like either romantic risk-free farming or high-tech "immaterial labor." By now, the exposés on the drudgery of call center work, not to mention the trauma-inducing labor of monitoring sites like Facebook for disturbing, illicit content, should have made the utter inadequacy of the idea of "immaterial labor" undeniable. The post-work imaginary likewise erases industry, manufacturing, the production and maintenance of infrastructure, and the care work necessary for social reproduction. Who is going to carry out the immense amount of labor required for responding to ever-increasing fires, droughts, storms, sea levels, and temperatures? Given that most cities are on coasts, the post-work cool-cities model either lacks the foresight necessary for responding to the changing climate or relies on a barely hidden genocidal imaginary, what we might call the Green Death.

Universal basic services

That capitalism and its bourgeois-liberal political and legal order are incapable of addressing the tasks of the present is not a radical observation. This view prevails right and left, as the rise of reactionary, authoritarian, and national conservativism across the globe continues to demonstrate. From time to time, especially in Latin America, left governments come to power, their range of action constrained by US imperialism and globalized neoliberalism. In the Global North, the left continues to be politically weak, either practically or dispositionally compelled to compromise with the liberal center protecting capitalism.

No tears should be shed for the end of the order that was supposed to have triumphed after the fall of the Berlin Wall. We can celebrate the fact that we no longer have to think in terms of capitalist compromise or take capitalism for granted: capitalism is destroying itself. Our task is to understand this process of destruction—the new dynamics of accumulation— and identify sites of strength and avenues of possibility for building communism instead of acquiescing to neofeudalism. Three dimensions of our present can shape a path toward a communist future: climate change as our general condition, universal basic services (UBS) as an economic vision, and the servant sector as the labor vanguard.

Everybody knows that we have to deal with climate change. Temperatures and species loss are rising, extreme weather is increasing, and there's no getting around it. At a minimum, fossil fuels have to be kept in the ground—despite the fact that the US and other governments are trying to shift the conversation from climate change to energy security. But the project of energy transition demands more than new sources of energy and practices of consumption. As planning replaces profit and we restructure production and consumption globally, we have to find spaces for meaningful life and work for the millions whose livelihoods have depended on the carbon economy. Failing on this score is a recipe for a deeper climate catastrophe or a deeper climate catastrophe plus fascism. The former points us to countries whose debt or level of development chain them to fossil fuel export or use. So long as imperialism dictates conditions of trade, these countries have no other choice but to produce for global export. The latter path of catastrophe plus fascism indexes the intensification of reactionary politics. Right-wing politicians channel outrage against anything green, environmental, or redolent of climate justice through tried-and-true insinuations of a theft of enjoyment: the left is coming to take your jobs, your way of life, your history, and your freedom.[19]

Communists should place the provision of universal basic services at the core of our vision for the post-capitalist future.[20] Reindustrializing is not a serious option: the environmental costs for such a strategy on a global scale are far too high. A more promising path toward economic viability comes from services. As Dylan Riley writes, "What the planet and humanity need is massive investment in low-return, low-productivity activities: care, education and environmental restoration."[21] In most so-called developed countries, education, transportation, and health care are widely recognized as services government is expected to provide. Most also presume some degree of public cultural support and provision—libraries, museums, and the arts—as well as state protection of natural resources in the form of greenspaces, parks, waterways, wetlands, and nature preserves. That people have a right to expect these basic public services is an unsurprising, familiar idea.

Neoliberal privatization schemes undermined public services ideationally as well as materially. Structural adjustment policies in the Global South in the 1980s and "shock treatment" in the former socialist bloc in the 1990s demolished public provision of vital services. In the capitalist countries of the Global North, free-market ideologists insisted that private ownership was more efficient. They convinced tax-payers that the costs of public provisioning were too high and that individuals should choose where their money is spent (a scheme that is never applied to endless war, but that's another story). Overall, governments were starved and states indebted. The possibilities for collective flourishing seemingly within the reach of so many, both north and south, in the middle of the last century collapsed under the weight of imperialist neoliberal globalization.

We have to take back, reinvigorate, and extend the promise of UBS as the post-capitalist basis for social and ecological flourishing. Under communism, public staffing and funding of such services will employ the millions released from the carbon, consumerist, commodity economy. People will be retrained with an eye toward infrastructural repair, wetland maintenance, land reclamation, forestry, and agroecology. UBS will solve the crises of the hinterlands, reknitting social ties and engaging ever more people in socially necessary repro-ductive labor: nursing, teaching, cooking, eldercare, and childminding. Rather than servants of tech lords, we will serve each other and hence the well-being of all—from each accord-ing to ability, to each according to need. Within a planned economy, services can and will scale, extending beyond frag-mented subcultures and functioning as universal guarantees.

Communists—and everyone else seeking a path toward an emancipatory egalitarian future on our warming planet—should recognize service-sector workers as the vanguard of the UBS struggle. Just as Marx and Engels merged the working-class struggle with the struggle for socialism, so must we knit together the economic struggles of service workers with the political task of building communism. Over the past decade, doctors, nurses, teachers, librarians, warehouse work-ers, trash collectors, transportation workers, baristas, adjunct professors, and graduate students have been leading the class struggle all over the world. Domestic workers in India,

Indonesia, and the US have organized to demand basic labor protections.[22] In the fall of 2023, daycare workers in Ireland, baggage handlers in Italy, hotel workers in Los Angeles, and nurses across six US states were just some of those in services carrying out labor strikes.[23] We have to follow their lead, recognizing their struggles as carrying within them the promise and potential for a world economy orientated toward common flourishing.

The general category of services is stratified and differentiated. Not all service work is paid. And not all service work is socially necessary, as many of those trapped in what David Graeber calls "bullshit jobs" would be the first to say. When Marx was writing, there was immense variety and differentiation among the crafts, tasks, and skills that rising capitalism was concentrating, mechanizing, and transforming. He could see the underlying commonality in the production of value, value that capitalists claimed for themselves. What we should see in the rise of the service sector is the subversion of capitalist value. Just like unpaid domestic labor, much of this work—not all—is unproductive from capital's standpoint but nonetheless useful and necessary for social reproduction. Its aim isn't private profit; it's meeting needs.

Jason E. Smith's analysis of the specific power of US teachers' strikes in 2019 is helpful for theorizing the political potential of organized service workers. For one, their power is "attributable not to their place in the technical division of labor but to their place within the social division of labor, since the withdrawal of their labor compels the interruption of work across a given locale."[24] An industrial work stoppage forces capitalists to negotiate by bringing production to a halt; if the factory owner wants to make a profit, production has to continue. When teachers strike, it's not just the work of education that comes to a halt. The impact extends as parents and caregivers have to scramble to find childcare, often having to take off work themselves. Teachers' strikes are self-generalizing (in ways that strikes in higher education, for example, are not). For another, teachers' strikes have a directly political content. The 2019 teachers' strikes "represented a spirited defense of the public sector as a cost necessary for the reproduction of society."[25] Teachers strike not just for their own good but for the good of their students. When they demand smaller class sizes, greater educational resources, school nurses, and an improvement of working conditions, they are fighting for the betterment of society more broadly, resisting the initiatives that undermine education for poor and working-class students and give upper-class households more excuses for retreating into private enclaves.

As sites for labor struggles, few services have this same self-generalizing-plus-public-good "double whammy." Transportation strikes come close. They can self-generalize insofar as people can't get to work, thereby expanding the strike, and they can make apparent the necessity of transportation for social reproduction. Nurses' strikes don't easily generalize beyond specific hospitals and clinics, even as they are clearly struggles in which the public has a significant stake. People need reliable care from competent medical professionals and want to avoid needless pain and suffering. Employers want employees healthy enough to show up for work. Strikes of warehouse and hotel workers can bring specific operations to a halt, but don't easily generalize beyond themselves, although they can inconvenience those whose work depends on particular supplies (such as those in the building trades) or gatherings (like conferences and conventions).

Given the disparity among services with respect to the power their labor action can potentially command, Smith is skeptical about the future of class struggle. He's especially attuned to the way that hinterlandization itself operates as a limit to the self-generalizing power of service-sector strikes: in areas from which capital has already withdrawn, whose infrastructures have already been dismantled, people are an expendable surplus. Smith writes:

> Today the children and grandchildren of these surplus people remain trapped in collapsing cities, far-flung suburbs, and rural ruins. They scrape by on part-time precarious work and tenuous lines of extortionate credit, commuting to and from work an hour each way, surveilled by heavily armed cops as they make their way home from bus stops. Some run rackets and hustles, while others sink into depression or drugs. Prison is always near.[26]

In the hinterlands, strikes of service workers may be harder to generalize because the people, the area, have already been written off. Nobody really cares if hospitals, schools, stores, and agencies close down; that's the way things were going anyway.

Smith leaves open another path as he describes the revolts of the *gilets jaunes* occurring in France around the same time as the transportation strikes: struggles in the hinterlands that don't take the form of labor actions. Located in key points in neither the social nor the technical division of labor, the *gilets jaunes* demonstrations tended to be disorganized and limited to Saturdays. With most of the protestors coming from "a world of insecure employment, rural poverty, and increasing inequality," their demonstrations targeted the inequity of France's fuel tax. The poor were being required to make sacrifices while corporations and wealthy urbanites were not.[27] This French struggle resonates with those in the US hinterlands where poor and working-class people feel—rightly or not—that they are forced to bear burdens that the privileged avoid: protests in rural communities against zoning, masks, vaccines, and gun laws; organized defense of the police (Blue Lives Matter); opposition to immigrants and refugees; and efforts to eliminate "controversial" books from public libraries (librarians have emerged as fierce defenders of readers and books in the face of this onslaught).

In the hinterlands, class struggle often takes the form not of a labor struggle but of a social-reproduction struggle. Rent strikes, cost of living demonstrations, and protests against raising the retirement age and increasing bus and subway fares are all class struggles. And even as the struggles in the hinterlands appear to be those of the surplus of the surplus, they have national impact. Throughout the US, Canada, the UK, and the EU a rightward political march is driven by the growing anger of the hinterland's dispossessed. This shift to the right isn't inevitable. It's about organizing, offering a politics, interpreting grievance, and imagining a future.

The decline and abandonment driving hinterlandization gives the hinterlands its place in the neofeudal landscape: they are sites for call centers, enormous warehouses ("fulfillment centers"), server farms, pipelines, energy and transportation hubs, and landfills and dumps. These are the sites that make possible consumption in the urban core, forgotten but indispensable. None is immune to sabotage, bombing, or blockade. Whether there are people who refuse to live in the old way, and whether there are enough people who feel that political struggle can usher in a new way, is a matter of organizing. When the left concentrates on the cities, the hinterlands become vassals of the right. The right promises to protect them, to build the walls, fund the police, and secure the weapons they imagine as vital to their defense.

Nothing is set in stone, especially as increasing numbers of people are forced to migrate to survive. The only certainty is that struggles will intensify, not the direction they will go. This is where the left has to fight: to provide a vision of future flourishing. UBS is key to this vision: health, education, parks, and libraries; regenerated environments and rebuilt infrastructures. Such services aren't handouts; they are suppositions for life and work on a warming planet.

There is a practical material reality behind recognizing service workers as the vanguard of the class struggle. Services are the sector where employment is increasing. Across the globe, job growth is in services, especially personal services. This creates a problem for capitalism because of services' challenge to the value form. Much of this work exceeds value; ill-suited to commodification, it fails to be confined within the terms of the capitalist circulation of value. As Gabriel Winant writes of healthcare workers: they are "collectively indispensable yet individually disposable."[28] The use value of care work is immeasurable even as it rarely commands an exchange value sufficient for its own reproduction. That this work is necessary for life but insufficient for capital accumulation is already spelling the end of capitalism: faced with growing service economies, asset holders rely on non-capitalist accumulation strategies. The strategy for communists has to be accepting and furthering the end of capitalism while championing crucial service work, especially that which is indispensable to social and ecological reproduction.

A society in which most labor is in services is oriented toward meeting needs. At present, as capital's own dynamics are coming under laws of motion no longer recognizably capitalist, these needs are configured within the social manor: the many serve the few. Those who work from home depend on deliveries from those who don't, on those whose working conditions deprive them of access to essentials like toilets. That the current capitalist economy is, like the old feudal one, oriented around the consumption needs of the lords creates specific contradictions. In the US, for example, there are shortages of nurses even as hospitals are closed. During COVID-19, clinics nurturing the vanities of the rich laid off their medical personnel while doctors and nurses at overcrowded hospitals got infected and died. We all know the contradictions around housing: massive shortages in affordable apartments while a global class of asset holders buys up everything it can. Just like public transportation before it, the conditions of air travel decline—not just delays and cancellations but growing numbers of near-miss collisions—as the rich fly above it all in their private planes. Services are meeting the needs of those who can pay, while those of us who can't are denied them.

Because those who can pay pay so much, because their consumption is excessive, unlimited, they are disproportionately responsible for the climate catastrophe. According to a 2022 Oxfam report, the carbon footprint of one of the richest billionaires is over a million times that of someone in the bottom 90 percent.[29] The social manor is the political and economic form that the environmental crisis is taking. From super yachts and private islands, land-hoarding and asset hiding, to investment in the corporations driving up carbon emissions, billionaire neofeudal lords are bringing the entire world to its knees.

Ending the domination of the asset holders and tech lords, eliminating the very existence of a billionaire class, is crucial for the flourishing of people and the planet. Service workers are the vanguard of this struggle. The strikes and struggles of nurses and teachers; of sanitation, transportation, warehouse, and domestic workers; and of renters, debtors, pensioners, and students points toward the imperative of universalizing basic services. Health, housing, and education are basic rights, not privileges of the few.

The subject supposed to fight

Universal basic services securing the conditions for social reproduction on a warming planet should be the economic and political horizon for working-class struggle today. Together with the long-held communist goals of abolishing private property and replacing the profit motive with planning, an emphasis on universal services imagines a communist path untethered from the industrial and developmentalist assumptions of the twentieth century. Capitalism is changing, and the orientation I suggest here responds to these changes.

Given the heterogeneity of the service sector, it wouldn't be accurate to say that this is the spontaneous orientation of all service workers, although the emergence of an ever-growing discourse on care is worth noting. Rather, this political orientation has to be brought in from the outside, as Lenin so scandalously said. A party of organizers, the communist party, can use this orientation to link and intensify the struggles. Instead of being servants in the social manor, service workers—including those who do informal and unpaid labor—can be hailed as the collective force ushering in a communist economy based on meeting needs not making profits. Just as their work ruptures capitalist value, so can their politics push the revolutionary transformation of society in a communist direction. Service work becomes not just indispensable to social reproduction. It acquires world-historical meaning as the force that can usher in communism.

The struggle against neofeudalism is a political struggle against the class of landlords, financiers, and asset holders exploiting, expropriating, and oppressing the rest of us. No one can fight this battle alone. The ruling class knows this: that's why they hire armies of lawyers and lobbyists; indeed, it's why they use the armed forces of the state. Not one billionaire could do anything alone (they are the most dependent of all). Those on the left need to abandon romantic misconceptions of individual efficacy and accept once again the necessity of cohering into an organized political force with a capacity to endure. This force is the party, the militant combination of comrades on the same side of the struggle for communism. When the party is strong, when its cadre is disciplined, people see it as fighting on their behalf. They aren't exposed and alone; others are willing to defend them. People's courage and the party's strength grow and intensify each other.

Expanding courage expands capacity, bringing the possibility of communism closer than it was before.

Rosa Luxemburg famously posed the alternative of socialism or barbarism. Our options now are communism or neofeudalism. If we don't fight for communism, we will end up in neofeudalism. That is the direction society is tending after forty years of neoliberalism. Standing in place, maintaining the status quo, is not an option. Fortunately, capitalism's own contradictions indicate a way forward and the class that can lead it: the class of service workers oriented toward securing the conditions under which people and the planet will thrive.

Notes

Introduction: Capital's Grave

1. Karl Marx and Friedrich Engels, *The Communist Manifesto*, trans. Samuel Moore in cooperation with Friedrich Engels (Pluto Press, 2017 [originally published in 1848; English translation 1888]), 69.
2. McKenzie Wark, *Capital Is Dead* (Verso, 2019).
3. Corey Robin, *The Reactionary Mind*, 2nd ed. (Oxford University Press, 2018), 30.
4. Ibid., 54.
5. Ibid., 191.
6. Rahmane Idrissa, "Mapping the Sahel," *New Left Review* 132 (November/December 2021).
7. Ibid.
8. For an account of the persistence of feudal governance in labor relations in the United States, see Karen Orren, *Belated Feudalism* (Cambridge University Press, 1991). For an account of the persistence of feudal values and practices in the nineteenth-century US, see Robert Yusef Rabiee, *Medieval America* (University of Georgia Press, 2020).
9. Ellen Meiksins Wood, *The Origin of Capitalism: A Longer View* (Verso, 2017), 7.
10. Ibid., 3.
11. Cédric Durand, "Scouting Capital's Frontiers," *New Left Review* 136 (July/August 2022); Yanis Varoufakis, *Technofeudalism* (The Bodley Head, 2023). I am grateful to Panos Tsoukalis for his gift of the latter.

12. Jaron Lanier, *You Are Not a Gadget* (Knopf, 2010).

13. Bruce Schneier, "You Have No Control over Security on the Feudal Internet," *Harvard Business Review*, June 6, 2013.

14. Jason E. Smith, *Smart Machines and Service Work* (Reaktion Books, 2020).

15. Karl Marx, *Capital*, vol. 1, trans. Ben Fowkes (Penguin, 1976), 574.

16. Already by the 1960s sociologists were observing the shift toward services in the advanced economies. In the years following the Second World War, the United States became the first economy in which over half of the employed workforce was not involved in the production of tangible goods. Victor R. Fuchs, *The Service Economy* (National Bureau of Economic Research, 1968), 1.

17. Quoted in Emily Badger, "Beverly Hills, Buckhead, Soho: The New Sites of Urban Unrest," *New York Times*, June 2, 2020, nytimes.com.

18. Emily Badger and Alicia Parlapiano, "The Rich Cut Their Spending. That Has Hurt All the Workers Who Count on It," *New York Times*, June 17, 2020, nytimes.com.

19. Aaron Benanav, *Automation and the Future of Work* (Verso, 2020), 56.

20. "Proportions of Economic Sectors in the Gross Domestic Product (GDP) in Selected Countries in 2023," statista.com, July 12, 2024. I am grateful to Lexy Funk for her research on this point.

21. "Share of Economic Sectors in the Gross Domestic Product (GDP) of Selected Global Regions in 2023," statista.com, July 12, 2024. Thanks to Lexy Funk for her research.

22. David Oks and Henry Williams, "The Long, Slow Death of Global Development," *American Affairs* 6, no. 4 (Winter 2022).

23. Brett Christophers, *Rentier Capitalism* (Verso, 2020).

24. Richard Westra, *Periodizing Capitalism and Capitalist Extinction* (Palgrave Macmillan, 2019), 221.

25. Ibid.

26. Katherine V. Stone and Robert Kuttner, "The Rise of Neo-Feudalism," *American Prospect*, April 8, 2020, prospect.org.

27. Katharina Pistor, *The Code of Capital* (Princeton University Press, 2019), 118.

28. Albena Azmanova, *Capitalism on Edge* (Columbia University Press, 2020).

29. Brett Christophers, *Our Lives in Their Portfolios* (Verso, 2023).

30. Yann Moulier Boutang, *Cognitive Capitalism*, trans. Ed Emery (Polity, 2011); Dan Schiller, *Digital Capitalism* (MIT Press, 1999); Jodi Dean, "Communicative Capitalism: Circulation and the Foreclosure of Politics," *Cultural Politics* 1, no. 1 (2005); Nick Srnicek, *Platform Capitalism* (Polity, 2017); Shoshana Zuboff, *The Age of Surveillance Capitalism* (Public Affairs, 2019).

31. Tim Di Muzio, *Carbon Capitalism* (Rowman and Littlefield, 2015); Andreas Malm, *Fossil Capital* (Verso, 2016); Jason W. Moore, "The Capitalocene, Part I: On the Nature and Origins of Our Ecological Crisis," *Journal of Peasant Studies* 44, no. 3 (2017).

32. Slavoj Žižek, *Violence* (Picador, 2008), 24.

33. Gérard Duménil and Dominique Lévy, *Capital Resurgent*, trans. Derek Jeffers (Harvard University Press, 2004); Robert Brenner, "Escalating Plunder," *New Left Review* 123 (May/June 2020).

34. Susan Reynolds, *Fiefs and Vassals: The Medieval Evidence Reconsidered* (Oxford University Press, 1994).

35. Joseph R. Strayer, *On the Medieval Origins of the Modern State* (Princeton University Press, 1970), 14.

36. Raymond Williams, *The Country and the City* (Oxford University Press, 1973), 35.

37. Joel Kotkin, *The New Class Conflict* (Telos Press, 2014), and *The Coming of Neo-feudalism* (Encounter Books, 2020).

38. I owe this point to discussions of the Crypto-Feudalism Working Group organized by Owen Marshall and including David Golumbia and Britt Paris.

39. Quoted in Badger, "Beverly Hills, Buckhead, Soho."

40. Care Collective, *The Care Manifesto* (Verso, 2020).

1 What the *Grundrisse* Tells Us about Uber

1. Kathleen Ronayne, "California Democrats Turn Up Pressure on Gig Economy," AP News, July 10, 2019, apnews.com.

2. Ellen Meiksins Wood, *The Origin of Capitalism: A Longer View* (Verso, 2017), 31.

3. Ibid., 36.

4. Karl Marx, *Capital*, vol. 1, trans. Ben Fowkes (Penguin, 1976), 799.

5. Evgeny Morozov, "Critique of Techno-feudal Reason," *New Left Review* 133/134 (January/April 2022).

6. Cédric Durand, "Scouting Capital's Frontiers," *New Left Review* 136 (July/August 2022).

7. William Clare Roberts, *Marx's Inferno: The Political Theory of Capital* (Princeton University Press, 2016), 207.

8. Harry Harootunian, *Marx after Marx: History and Time in the Expansion of Capitalism* (Columbia University Press, 2015), 9.

9. Morozov, "Critique of Techno-feudal Reason," 126.

10. Wood, *Origin of Capitalism*.

11. Morozov, "Critique of Techno-feudal Reason," 126.

12. Ibid., 98.

13. Brett Christophers, *Rentier Capitalism* (Verso, 2020), xviii.

14. Ibid., xviii.

15. Robert Brenner, "Behind the Economic Turbulence," interview by Suzi Weissman, *Against the Current*, May–June 2019, againstthecurrent.org.

16. Ibid.

17. Ibid.

18. Aaron Benanav, "A Dissipating Glut?," *New Left Review* 140/141 (May/June 2023).

19. David Oks and Henry Williams, "The Long, Slow Death of Global Development," *American Affairs* 6, no. 4 (Winter 2022).

20. Ibid.

21. Uber, *A Better Deal: Partnering to Improve Platform Work for All* (Uber, 2021), 11.

22. Judgment: Uber BV and others (Appellants) v Aslam and others (Respondents), Hilary Term [2021] UKSC 5, on appeal from: [2018] EWCA Civ 2748 (19 February 2021), 22.

23. Kellen Browning, "California Court Mostly Upholds Prop. 22 in Win for Uber and Other Gig Companies," *New York Times,* March 13, 2023, nytimes.com.

24. Michael Hiltzik, "Uber Reneges on the 'Flexibility' It Gave Drivers to Win Their Support for Proposition 22," *Los Angeles Times*, May 28, 2021, latimes.com.

25. V. B. Dubal, "An Uber Ambivalence: Employee Status, Worker Perspectives, and Regulation in the Gig Economy," UC Hastings Law Legal Studies Research Series, Research Paper 381 (November 2019), 15.

26. Mike Isaac, *Super Pumped: The Battle for Uber* (W. W. Norton and Company, 2019), 87–8.

27. Edward Ongweso Jr., "The Lockout: Why Uber Drivers in NYC Are Sleeping in Their Cars," *Vice*, March 19, 2020, vice.com.

28. Isaac, *Super Pumped*, 137.

29. Ibid., 82–3.

30. Ibid., 114.

31. Ibid., 115.

32. Hubert Horan, "Can Uber Ever Deliver? Part One—Understanding Uber's Bleak Operating Economics," *Naked Capitalism*, November 30, 2016, nakedcapitalism.com.

33. Hubert Horan, "Can Uber Ever Deliver? Part Twenty-One: Mike Isaac's Book Ignores Economics and Financial Results and Gets the Uber Story Almost Entirely Wrong," *Naked Capitalism*, September 16, 2019, nakedcapitalism.com.

34. Alex Rosenblat and Luke Stark, "Algorithmic Labor and Information Asymmetries: A Case Study of Uber's Drivers," *International Journal of Communication* 10 (2016): 3758–84.

35. Pat Garofalo, "California's Prop 22 Is Going to Screw Over Gig Workers for Years to Come, and the Terrible Anti-labor Policy Could Soon Be Coming to a State Near You," *Business Insider*, December 14, 2020, businessinsider.com.

36. Alexis C. Madrigal, "The Servant Economy," *Atlantic*, March 6, 2019, theatlantic.com.

37. Ibid.

38. Juliet B. Schor, *After the Gig* (University of California Press, 2020), 96.

39. Edward Ongweso Jr., "DoorDash Says Its Own Pay Model Is a Risk to Its Business in Public Filing," *Vice*, November 13, 2020, vice.com.

40. Karl Marx, *Grundrisse*, trans. Martin Nicolaus (Vintage Books, 1973), 496.

41. Karl Marx, *Pre-Capitalist Economic Formations*, trans. Jack Cohen (International Publishers, 1964), 94.

42. Marx, *Grundrisse*, 496.

43. Ibid., 499.

44. Marx, *Pre-Capitalist Economic Formations*, 95.

45. Ibid., 103.

46. Ibid., 87.

47. Ibid., 102.

48. Marx, *Capital*, vol. 1, 798.

49. Karl Marx, *Theories of Surplus Value*, vol. 1 (Pattern Books, 2020 [sourced from Progress Publishers, 1863]), 456.

50. Marx, *Grundrisse*, 503.

51. Ibid., 507.

52. Marx, *Theories of Surplus Value*, 484.

53. Hubert Horan, "Uber's Path of Destruction," *American Affairs* 3, no. 2 (Summer 2019): 108–33.

54. Ongweso, "The Lockout."

55. Marx, *Grundrisse*, 510.

56. Madrigal, "The Servant Economy."

57. Jeffery C. Mays, "New York Passes Sweeping Bills to Improve Conditions for Delivery Workers," *New York Times*, September 23, 2021, nytimes.com.

58. Yanis Varoufakis, *Technofeudalism* (The Bodley Head, 2023), 85.

59. Reeves Wiedeman, *Billion Dollar Loser* (Little, Brown and Company, 2020), 179.

60. Harootunian, *Marx after Marx*, 5.

2 Forward Can Be Backward

1. Representative contributions to the enormous Marxist literature
   on the transition from feudalism to capitalism include *The Transition from Feudalism to Capitalism*, introduced by Rodney
   Hilton (Verso, 1976); T. H. Aston and C. H. E. Philpin, eds., *The
   Brenner Debate: Agrarian Class Structure and Economic Development in Pre-Industrial Europe* (Cambridge University Press,
   1987); Ellen Meiksins Wood, *The Origin of Capitalism: A Longer
   View* (Verso, 2017); and Jairus Banaji, *A Brief History of
   Commercial Capitalism* (Haymarket, 2020). Discussions of the
   transition from capitalism to socialism are a mainstay of socialist
   and communist debate throughout the twentieth century. Particularly interesting for their rejections of socialism as a specific stage
   of communist development are Étienne Balibar, *On the Dictatorship of the Proletariat*, trans. Grahame Lock (NLB, 1977), and
   Antonio Negri, *Marx beyond Marx: Lessons on the Grundrisse*,
   trans. Harry Cleaver, Michael Ryan, and Maurizio Viano
   (Autonomedia, 1991). Alberto Toscano provides an insightful
   overview of Balibar's and Negri's contributions to the challenge
   of thinking transition, "Transition Deprogrammed," *South
   Atlantic Quarterly* 113, no. 4 (Fall 2014): 761–75.
2. In his November 1877 letter to the editor of *Otecestvenniye
   Zapisky*, Marx says that it is wrong to attribute to him a theory
   of the march of history. Karl Marx, "Letter from Marx to Editor
   of the *Otecestvenniye Zapisky*," Marx-Engels Correspondence
   1877, marxists.org.
3. Massimiliano Tomba's reworking of historical materialism's
   plural temporalities opens up the complexity of this undertak-
   ing, *Marx's Temporalities*, trans. Peter D. Thomas and Sara R.
   Farris (Haymarket Books, 2013).
4. Karl Marx, *Capital*, vol. 1, trans. Ben Fowkes (Penguin, 1976), 345.
5. Karl Marx, "The Eighteenth Brumaire of Louis Bonaparte,"
   Selected Writings, ed. Lawrence H. Simon (Hackett Publishing,
   1994), 188.

6. Letter from Engels to Marx, December 15, 1882; supplementary text included in Karl Marx, *Pre-capitalist Economic Formations*, introduced by Eric Hobsbawm (International Publishers, 1965), 146.

7. V. I. Lenin, *The State and Revolution*, 1917, ch. 5, available at marxists.org.

8. V. I. Lenin, *Imperialism: The Highest Stage of Capitalism*, 1916, ch. 7, available at marxists.org.

9. V. I. Lenin, *The Development of Capitalism in Russia*, 1899, ch. 3, part 2, available at marxists.org.

10. Rosa Luxemburg, *The Accumulation of Capital*, trans. Agnes Schwarzschild (Routledge, 2003), 346.

11. Ibid., 351.

12. Ibid., 350.

13. Feminists such as Maria Mies have highlighted nature and the family as "outsides" necessary for capitalist productivity. See *Patriarchy and Accumulation on a World Scale* (Zed Books, 1986).

14. Walter Rodney, *How Europe Underdeveloped Africa* (Verso, 2018), 12.

15. Ibid.

16. Ibid.

17. René Zavaleta Mercado, *Towards a History of the National-Popular in Bolivia, 1879–1980*, trans. Anne Freeland (Seagull Books, 2018), 188. I'm indebted to André Nascimento for encouraging me to engage this text.

18. Ibid., 113.

19. Ibid., 116.

20. Ibid., 128.

21. Ibid., 136.

22. Ibid.

23. Ibid., 138.

24. Ibid., 139.

25. Louis Althusser, *Philosophy of the Encounter*, trans. G. M. Goshgarian (Verso, 2006), 201. I'm indebted to Mark Ajita for bringing this to my attention.

26. Ibid., 203.

27. Jairus Banaji, *Theory as History* (Haymarket Books, 2011), esp. ch. 2.

28. Ibid., 92.

29. Ibid., 93, 65.

30. Ibid., 65.

31. Ibid., 62.

32. Ibid., 63.

33. Harry Harootunian, *Marx after Marx: History and Time in the Expansion of Capitalism* (Columbia University Press, 2015), 13.

34. See also Jason Read, *The Micro-Politics of Capital* (State University of New York Press, 2003).

35. Harootunian, *Marx after Marx*, 29.

36. Ibid., 5.

37. Ibid., 151.

38. Ibid., 163.

39. Ibid., 174.

40. Lenin, *State and Revolution*, ch. 5.

41. Balibar, *On the Dictatorship of the Proletariat*, 124.

42. Ibid., 134, italics in original.

43. Ibid., 135–6.

44. Ibid., 137.

45. Lenin, *Imperialism*, ch. 7.

46. Balibar, *On the Dictatorship of the Proletariat*, 140–1.

47. Ibid., 141.

48. Ibid., 140.

49. As Marx writes in his preface to *A Contribution to the Critique of Political Economy* (1859): "The bourgeois mode of production is the last antagonistic form of the social process of production—antagonistic not in the sense of individual antagonism but of an antagonism that emanates from the individuals' social conditions of existence—but the productive forces developing within bourgeois society create also the material conditions for a solution to this antagonism." Available at marxists.org.

50. Negri, *Marx beyond Marx*, 165.

51. Ibid., 142.

52. Antonio Negri, *Factory of Strategy: 33 Lessons on Lenin*, trans. Arianna Bove (Columbia University Press, 2004), 250.

53. Ibid., 257.

54. Negri, *Marx beyond Marx*, 153.

55. Ibid., 154.

56. Aaron Benanav, *Automation and the Future of Work* (Verso, 2020), 24. Robert Brenner, *The Economics of Global Turbulence* (Verso, 2006).

57. Étienne Balibar, "Elements for a Theory of Transition," in Louis Althusser et al., *Reading* Capital, trans. Ben Brewster (Verso, 2009), 343.

3 Neofeudalism's Basic Features

1. Antonio Negri, *The End of Sovereignty*, trans. Ed Emery (Polity, 2022), 31.

2. Ibid., 37.

3. Ibid., 61.

4. Quinn Slobodian, *Globalists* (Harvard University Press, 2018), 210, 222.

5. Ibid., 503.

6. Negri, *End of Sovereignty*, 92.

7. Ibid., 93.

8. Robert Brenner, "Escalating Plunder," *New Left Review* 123 (May/June 2020).

9. Negri, *End of Sovereignty*, 92.

10. Alain Supiot, "The Public-Private Relation in the Context of Today's Refeudalization," *International Journal of Constitutional Law* 11, no. 1 (2013): 140.

11. Ibid.

12. Ibid., 141.

13. Ibid., 139.

14. Ibid., 140.

15. Perry Anderson, *Passages from Antiquity to Feudalism* (Verso, 1996 [1974]), 147ff.

16. Ellen Meiksins Wood, *Citizens to Lords* (Verso, 2008), 167–8.

17. Ibid., 168.

18. Chiara Cordelli, *The Privatized State* (Princeton University Press, 2020), 11.

19. Quinn Slobodian, *Crack-Up Capitalism* (Metropolitan Books, 2023).

20. Katherine V. Stone and Robert Kuttner, "The Rise of Neo-feudalism," *American Prospect*, April 8, 2020, prospect.org.

21. Sohrab Ahmari, *Tyranny, Inc.* (Forum Books, 2023).

22. Alexander J. S. Colvin, "The Growing Use of Mandatory Arbitration," Economic Policy Institute, April 6, 2018, epi.org.

23. Manuel Perez-Rocha and Jen Moore, "Mining Companies Use Excessive Legal Powers to Gamble with Latin American Lives," *Truthout*, May 14, 2019, truthout.org.

24. Jayati Ghosh, "The Creation of the Next Imperialism," *Monthly Review*, July 1, 2015, monthlyreview.org.

25. Ibid.

26. Kevin P. Donovan and Emma Park, "Perpetual Debt in the Silicon Savannah," *Boston Review*, September 20, 2019, bostonreview.net.

27. Stone and Kuttner, "The Rise of Neo-feudalism."

28. Alan Bryden and Marina Caparini, eds., *Private Actors and Security Governance* (Geneva Centre for Security Sector Governance, 2006).

29. Marina Caparini, "Applying a Security Governance Perspective to the Privatization of Security," in Bryden and Caparini, *Private Actors and Security Governance*, 264.

30. Alexandra Natapoff, *Punishment without Crime* (Basic Books, 2018).

31. Manu Karuka, "Hunger Politics: Sanctions as Siege Warfare," in Stuart Davis and Immanuel Ness, eds., *Sanctions as War* (Brill, 2022), 51–62.

32. Jessica Whyte, "The Opacity of Economic Coercion," *LPE Project* (blog), June 21, 2023, lpeproject.org.

33. David Graeber, *Bullshit Jobs* (Simon and Schuster, 2018), 177–80.

34. Ibid., 191.

35. Derek Thompson, "Why Nerds and Nurses Are Taking Over the U.S. Economy," *Atlantic*, October 26, 2017, theatlantic.com.

36. Geraint Harvey et al., "Neo-villeiny and the Service Sector: The Case of Hyper Flexible and Precarious Work in Fitness Centres," *Work, Employment and Society* 31, no. 1 (2017): 19–35.

37. Corinne Redfern, "'I Want to Go Home': Filipina Domestic Workers Face Exploitative Conditions," *Guardian*, January 27, 2021, theguardian.com.

38. "Background Study on the Operations of the Extractive Industries Sector in Africa and Its Impacts on the Realisation of Human and Peoples' Rights under the African Charter on Human and Peoples' Rights," study prepared for the African Commission on Human and Peoples' Rights, adopted by the African Commission during its 33rd Extraordinary Session in July 2021, 15. Document on file with the author.

39. Ali Kadri, *Arab Development Denied* (Anthem Press, 2015), 3.

40. Ibid., 4.

41. Brett Christophers, *The New Enclosures* (Verso, 2018), 329.

42. Nick Srnicek, *Platform Capitalism* (Polity, 2017), 43.

43. Emily Guendelsberger, *On the Clock* (Little, Brown and Company, 2019), 22.

44. Stacy Mitchell, "Amazon's Toll Road," Institute for Local Self-Reliance, December 2021, ilsr.org.

45. Mary Zhang, "ChatGPT and OpenAI's Use of Azure's Cloud Infrastructure," Dgtl Infra, January 26, 2023, dgtlinfra.com.

46. Shoshana Zuboff, *The Age of Surveillance Capitalism* (Public Affairs, 2019), 386–8.

47. Wood, *Citizens to Lords*, 172.

48. Alec MacGillis, *Fulfillment* (Farrar, Straus and Giroux, 2021), 8.

49. Rowland Atkinson, *Alpha City: How London Was Captures by the Super-Rich* (Verso, 2020), 159.

50. Guendelsberger, *On the Clock*, 166.

51. Ibid., 25.

52. Philip G. Cerny, "Neomedievalism, Civil War and the New Security Dilemma: Globalisation as Durable Disorder," *Civil Wars* 1, no. 1 (February 1998): 45.

53. Ibid., 55.

54. Umair Haque, "Why the World Is Going Backwards—and How to Stop It," Medium, December 31, 2022, medium.com/eudaimonia-co.

55. Ruth Graham, "Christian Prophets Are on the Rise. What Happens When They Are Wrong?," *New York Times*, February 11, 2021, nytimes.com.

56. Bianca Bosker, "Why Witchcraft Is on the Rise," *Atlantic*, March 2020, theatlantic.com.

57. Quoted in Keith A. Spencer, "Revenge of the Nerd-Kings: Why Some in Silicon Valley Are Advocating for Monarchy," *Salon*, April 13, 2019, salon.com.

58. Corey Robin, *The Reactionary Mind* (Oxford University Press, 2011), 99–100.

59. Haque, "Why the World Is Going Backwards."

60. Darko Suvin, "Anti-Utopia in Coronisation Times: Capitalocene and Death," 2020, 6–7. Manuscript on file with author.

61. Darko Suvin, "How to Go On: Political Epistemology for Pandemy Times," *Socialism and Democracy* 34, nos. 2–3 (2020): 181–211.

62. Jacques Lacan, *Anxiety: The Seminar of Jacques Lacan, Book X*, trans. A. R. Price (Polity, 2014), 218.

63. Ibid., 77.

64. Ibid., 76.

65. Ibid., 54.

4 The Subject Supposed to Care

1. For background on the "See? Nobody cares" meme, see knowyourmeme.com.

2. Cathrin Schaer, "Why Would We Fight Somebody Else's War?," DW, April 23, 2022, dw.com.

3. Dustin Jones, "Co-owner of NBA's Warriors Slammed after Saying 'Nobody Cares about the Uyghurs,'" NPR, January 17, 2022, npr.org.

4. Alan Joseph Bauer, "The Palestinians: A People about Whom Nobody Cares," *Jewish Press*, October 3, 2023, jewishpress.com.

5. Raja Abdulrahim et al., "Israel Sending More Troops to Rafah amid Warnings of Famine in Gaza," *New York Times*, May 16, 2024, nytimes.com.

6. Marc Bloch, *Feudal Society*, vol. 1, trans. L. A. Manyon (University of Chicago Press, 1970), 72.

7. Darian Leader, *What Is Madness?* (Penguin Books, 2011), 74.

8. Ibid., 80.

9. Antony Lerman, *Whatever Happened to Antisemitism?* (Pluto Press, 2022), 15.

10. Barnaby Raine, "Jewphobia," *Salvage*, January 7, 2019, salvage .zone.

11. Faygie Holt, "Inside a US College Gaza Camp: 'No One Cares about How This Is Affecting Jewish Students,'" *Jewish Chronicle*, May 3, 2024, thejc.com.

12. "Melania Trump Says 'Don't Care' Jacket Was a Message," BBC News, October 13, 2018, bbc.com.

13. Slavoj Žižek, "The Interpassive Subject," *Traverses* (Centre George Pompidou, 1998), lacan.com.

14. Neil Bedi et al., "How Counterprotesters at U.C.L.A. Provoked Violence, Unchecked for Hours," *New York Times*, May 3, 2024, nytimes.com.

15. Ali Winston, "Why Far-Right Groups Are Disrupting US Campus Protests: 'When There's So Much Attention, They Show Up,'" *Guardian*, May 10, 2024, theguardian.com.

16. Bedi et al., "How Counterprotesters at U.C.L.A. Provoked Violence."

17. Paul Krugman, "The Perils of Plutocratic Pettiness," *New York Times*, May 23, 2022, nytimes.com.

18. Marc Bloch, *Feudal Society*, vol. 2, trans. L. A. Manyon (University of Chicago Press, 1970), 443.

19. Quoted in Andrew Cole, *The Birth of Theory* (University of Chicago Press, 2014), 79.

20. Jacques Lacan, *The Seminar of Jacques Lacan, Book III: The Psychoses 1955–1956*, trans. Russell Grigg (W. W. Norton and Company, 1993), 40.

21. Ibid., 39–40.

22. Mladen Dolar, "Lord and Bondsman on the Couch," *American Journal of Semiotics* 9, nos. 2–3 (1992): 69–90, 77.

23. Lacan, *Seminar of Jacques Lacan, Book III*, 87.

24. Ibid.

25. Jacques Lacan, *Anxiety: The Seminar of Jacques Lacan, Book X*, trans. A. R. Price (Polity, 2014), 77.

26. Ibid., 337.

27. For a compelling account of structure, see Anna Kornbluh, *Immediacy: Or, The Style of Too Late Capitalism* (Verso, 2024).

28. See my discussion in *Crowds and Party* (Verso, 2016).

29. See my discussion in *Comrade: An Essay on Political Belonging* (Verso, 2019).

Conclusion: The Servant Vanguard

1. Aaron Benanav, *Automation and the Future of Work* (Verso, 2020), 57–60.

2. Silvia Federici, *Revolution at Point Zero* (PM Press, 2012), 99.

3. Ibid., 99.

4. Silvia Federici, *Re-enchanting the World* (PM Press, 2018), 154. See also Federici, *Revolution at Point Zero*, 82.

5. Federici, *Revolution at Point Zero*, 92.

6. Silvia Federici, *Caliban and the Witch* (Autonomedia, 2004).

7. Federici, *Re-enchanting the World*, 164.

8. Raymond Williams, *The Country and the City* (Oxford University Press, 1973), 96ff.

9. Federici, *Re-enchanting the World*, 158.

10. Karl Marx, *Capital*, vol. 1, trans. Ben Fowkes (Penguin, 1976), 574–5.

11. Federici, *Revolution at Point Zero*, 95.

12. See Paul Burkett, *Marx and Nature* (Haymarket Books, 2014), and Kohei Saito, *Marx in the Anthropocene* (Cambridge University Press, 2022).

13. Karl Marx, *Capital*, vol. 3, trans. David Fernbach (Penguin, 1981), 959.

14. Karl Marx, *Grundrisse*, trans. Martin Nicolaus (Vintage Books, 1973), 706–8; Saito, *Marx in the Anthropocene*, 60–1.

15. Federici, *Revolution at Point Zero*, 101.

16. Ibid., 104.

17. Ibid., 147.

18. Alex Gurevitch, "Post-Work Socialism Is a Tempting Illusion," *Jacobin*, August 5, 2023, jacobin.com.

19. Slavoj Žižek, *Tarrying with the Negative* (Duke University Press, 1993), ch. 6.

20. Anna Coote and Andrew Percy, *The Case for Universal Basic Services* (Polity, 2020).

21. Dylan Riley, "Drowning in Deposits," *Sidecar*, April 4, 2023, newleftreview.org.

22. Ben O'Donovan-Iland, "Domestic Workers in India Are Demanding Justice," Institute of Development Studies, August 16, 2023, ids.ac.uk; Niniek Karmini, "Indonesian Protesters Begin Hunger Strike as Bill to Protect Domestic Workers Stalls in Parliament," AP News, August 14, 2023, apnews.com; Rafael Bernal, "Domestic Workers Are Organizing for Better Working Conditions Nationwide," *Hill*, July 9, 2023, thehill.com.

23. Sarah Horgan, "'Horrifying to Hear What Childcare Workers Are Dealing With': Cork Councillor Concern over Impact of Practitioners Strike," *Echo Live*, September 13, 2023, echolive .ie; Giovanni Legorano, "Italy's Airport Baggage Handlers Set to Take 24-Hour Strike on Friday," Anadolu Agency, September 27, 2023, aa.com.tr; Suhauna Hussain, "After Three Months of Rolling Strikes, Second L.A. Hotel Reaches Tentative Agreement with Union," *Los Angeles Times*, September 29, 2023, latimes .com; Kate Gibson, "Kaiser Permanente Workers Launch Massive

Strike over Staffing and Pay," CBS News, October 4, 2023, cbsnews.com.

24. Jason E. Smith, *Smart Machines and Service Work* (Reaktion Books, 2020), 145.

25. Ibid., 141.

26. Ibid., 148.

27. Ben Martin, "Green Hearts and Gilets Jaunes," Green Economy Coalition, March 22, 2019, greeneconomycoalition.org.

28. Gabriel Winant, *The Next Shift* (Harvard University Press, 2021), 261.

29. Alex Maitland et al., *Carbon Billionaires: The Investment Emissions of the World's Richest People*, Oxfam Briefing Note (Oxfam, November 2022), 3, oxfamamerica.org.

Index